Joyful Learning

T0383569

Joyful Learning: Tools to Infuse Your 6–12 Classroom with Meaning, Relevance, and Fun is a guide for teachers seeking to energize their practice and deeply engage students. Author Stephanie Farley shows how to create student-centered learning experiences that immerse students in meaning, relevance, and joy. She shows how you can foster student engagement and motivation with a combination of choice, challenge, and play, thereby improving learning outcomes.

Practical strategies are included in each chapter, such as how to write rubrics that foster effective feedback, how to incorporate performance and competency-based assessment, and how to have students grade themselves through a process of self-evaluation and reflection. Throughout, she offers tools such as targets and rubrics, checklists to guide planning, and prompts that help you apply the ideas to your own assignments and assessments.

With the book's specific, immediately applicable examples, you'll be able to help your students feel connected to the lessons, happy about their progress, and joyfully engaged in the learning process.

Stephanie Farley is a writer and consultant working with schools and teachers on issues of curriculum, assessment, instruction, SEL, and building relationships. She is a former English teacher and independent school administrator and has served as a member of California Association of Independent School accreditation teams.

Also Available from Routledge Eye on Education

www.routledge.com/k-12

Passionate Learners, 3e: How to Engage and Empower Your Students
Pernille Ripp

Motivating Struggling Learners: 10 Ways to Build Student Success
Barbara R. Blackburn

The Student Motivation Handbook: Fifty Ways to Boost an Intrinsic Desire to Learn
Larry Ferlazzo

Working Hard, Working Happy
Rita Platt

Learner Choice, Learner Voice: A Teacher's Guide to Promoting Agency in the Classroom
Ryan L Schaaf, Becky Zayas, Ian Jukes

Joyful Learning

Tools to Infuse Your 6–12 Classroom with Meaning, Relevance, and Fun

Stephanie Farley

Routledge
Taylor & Francis Group

NEW YORK AND LONDON

Designed cover image: © Getty Images

First published 2023
by Routledge
605 Third Avenue, New York, NY 10158

and by Routledge
4 Park Square, Milton Park, Abingdon, Oxon, OX14 4RN

Routledge is an imprint of the Taylor & Francis Group, an informa business

© 2023 Stephanie Farley

ISBN: 978-1-032-44993-7 (hbk)
ISBN: 978-1-032-44630-1 (pbk)
ISBN: 978-1-003-37490-9 (ebk)

DOI: 10.4324/9781003374909

Typeset in Palatino
by codeMantra

To all the teachers who've generated a sense of what's possible, especially Mrs. Welch, my 6th grade English teacher, who read my story "Lady Challenger" and asked me if I had more stories she could read.

Figure D.1 Author of "Lady Challenger" in 6th Grade. Author's photograph.

Contents

About the Author

A former English teacher and independent school administrator, Stephanie Farley is a writer and consultant working with schools and teachers on issues of curriculum, assessment, instruction, SEL, and building relationships. She has served as a member of California Association of Independent School accreditation teams and learned about competency-based assessment in her role as a site director for the Mastery Transcript Consortium.

An avid reader, Stephanie tends to choose stories about detectives, moms, and time travelers. As a highly amateur baker, Stephanie appreciates baking projects in her zone of proximal development, such as two-layer cakes and no-knead bread. She lives in Los Angeles with her husband, two daughters, and adoring dog.

1

Joyful Approach

I am one of those people who has always liked school. I mean, I got bored sometimes, but, in general, I liked learning and I liked knowing things. Though I wasn't as smart, organized, or dedicated as Hermione Granger, I acted like I was, annoying the people around me. While it came as somewhat of a surprise to me that I became a secondary teacher, it didn't surprise anyone else, as I was always trying to school my friends and family about the perils of eating meat, the theories of Carl Jung, or the proper way to use hot rollers.

I was a mostly uncritical consumer of education. I loved my English classes unconditionally because I got to read and write. Memorization got me through most other classes, and, when it didn't, I simply had to figure out what the teacher wanted and deliver it. Geometry and calculus challenged this notion, but it wasn't until college that I truly realized learning was about more than following instructions. I almost failed Psychology of Learning because I couldn't figure out what the professor wanted. My papers weren't clear enough; my reasoning wasn't rigorous enough; and my experiments were ludicrous. I got through it, but I was bruised and left wondering what on earth was wrong with that professor? Why was he so cranky? Upon reflection, I understood that particular professor was an effective teacher, as he forced an experimentation from me that I wasn't used to but ultimately served me well.

I started teaching 6th graders one month after I finished graduate school. I wasn't trained to be a teacher; I had a bachelor's degree in psychology and a master's degree in English literature. I became a teacher because my previous

DOI: 10.4324/9781003374909-1

plan of being a professor was scuttled by a chance conversation with the English department chair at an Ivy League university. She visited my school and, as a graduate student, I was invited to a special lecture with her. I asked her about jobs when school was done. She said there were no jobs for English PhDs, and we'd all be better off thinking of other ways to use our humanities education. This really stuck in my brain. I already owed a ton of money in student loans, and I didn't want to go into more debt only to find myself jobless when I was finally done with school. One of my friends had trained to be a teacher and she told me that I could always teach high school English in a private school, as at the time a teaching credential wasn't required in private high schools.

By the time I finished graduate school, I was connected to the independent school world through another contact. The job that was available to me was teaching a summer school class for rising 7th graders. I thought, "Why not?" and took the job. I don't remember much about what happened, but I know I tried to teach the kids *Romeo and Juliet.* And, while I failed miserably at the teaching part, I loved it! I liked hanging out with the kids, trying to get them to enjoy Shakespeare. I enjoyed the pressure of preparing a lesson every day. I even appreciated the schedule. It all appealed to me.

After my summer of Shakespeare with 6th graders, I got a job teaching high school students. I had three preps: World History, AP Literature, and Algebra II. Again, I had no idea what I was doing. I learned all the content the night before I taught it, and I could only teach history and algebra one way. I use "content" here intentionally: I wasn't teaching skills, as I didn't know enough about history or math to appreciate what those skills might be. If the kids didn't understand the material the way I learned and then presented it, we were all stuck. Fortunately for those kids and for me, the next year I got a job teaching 7th grade English at a different school. I had found my calling.

As I started my teaching career in earnest, I strove to replicate what I felt were the "rigorous" elements of my own education. For English, this comprised note-taking, considering themes as conflicts (i.e., "desire vs. responsibility"), and writing persuasive essays about those themes. Whether this was appropriate for 7th graders or not, it was what I knew from my own recent college experience, so I marched forward. I was a pleasant person, but I was a *terrible* teacher. Let me explain.

I gave bi-weekly "vocabulary" quizzes. There were five words on each quiz, taken from the novels the kids read. The kids had to know how to spell the word properly, know the definition, and use the word in a sentence. I took off points for spelling, points for incorrect definitions, points for incorrect usage, and points for improper punctuation. It was a trainwreck! Some nice mom tried to help me understand the error of my ways, but I rationalized away her calm explanations and continued on my misguided and harmful path in the name of rigor.

I gave grammar quizzes that everyone failed. I'd give re-tests and average the two grades together, on the advice of a teacher who was older and wiser than me. My stomach hurts just thinking about this.

The essays I assigned were esoteric – way above the kids' heads, most of the time – and I had not heard of a rubric, so I didn't have one. I want to be clear with you and with myself...I essentially made up the grades. My process was to read all the essays, find the most well-written, compellingly argued one, give that an A, and then I figured out the rest of the grades from there. I knew I was looking for a clear, one-sided thesis and textual evidence, but let's be real...I was making it up, just as my teachers and professors had done when I was a student. I should point out that my school used a grading scale, with ranges equaling certain letter grades. So 89.5%–92% was an A-. The notion that I could articulate the difference between 92% and 93% is pretty ludicrous: I couldn't then and I can't now. The numbers I assigned were based on the letter grade I wanted to assign the paper, not the other way around. There was no adding up of points to get an 83 or an 85. It was just a B.

Lastly, I didn't have clear intentions about what I was teaching. By this I mean, I was teaching books, and I wanted the kids to understand plot, character, and theme, but I didn't sit down to ask myself "what are the skills I want to see the kids develop and how exactly am I building those skills with these materials?"

I was a terrible teacher when I first started because I didn't have a background in educational principles. I didn't know about all the wonderful tools teachers have at their disposal (i.e., backwards planning, formative assessment, summative assessment of just a few targeted skills, conferences, retests for an entirely new grade) and the research that helped teachers understand effective instruction. I was well into my teaching career when I encountered the educational research and methodology that came to define my practice and that I now call "joyful learning".

Each year, I grew a little less terrible as a teacher. I learned through experience what worked and what didn't with both 7th and 8th graders. Some of my students thrived, but others languished, and I took that personally. My goal became not only to help every student find success in English class, but also to make it the class every kid looked forward to in their day. I studied pedagogy. I visited other schools and observed the cool and varied ways teachers captured their students' interest. I read about brain research, how to teach reading, and constructivism. I took classes from various educational bodies and read books written by the most engaging presenters. All the while, I continued to teach and experiment on my students.

And then, one year, my experiments paid off with a breakthrough in my own understanding and in the experience of my students. Here was my epiphany: people learn through *memorization* and *experiences*. I had been too focused on memorization, so I decided to shift to experiences. For quite some time, I hadn't realized that it was possible to create learning experiences in the discipline of English. Learning experiences were for science or art…you know, subjects in which you could do stuff with your own two hands: mold clay, or measure ingredients in a beaker, or examine the insides of a cow eye-ball. But, I reasoned, if my goal was for students to be able to make connections between the book, themselves, and the greater world, then I'd have to give them an avenue to do that. I recognize now this is all fairly obvious, but this simple truth eluded me for years of teaching! From then on, I considered how to provide learning experiences that allowed students to draw their own conclusions about themes in the book. An example that I remember from that breakthrough year – about 12 years into my teaching career – is that I was teaching *Macbeth*, and I wanted the students to understand the burden of Macbeth that one of the kids had mentioned in a discussion. So I had my students pick up their heavy backpacks and instructed them to march around the field outside, holding the backpack. This took about seven minutes. When we returned to the classroom, I asked the kids why I would have them tramp around carrying heavy books and what it had to do with Macbeth. The student who had mentioned the burden of Macbeth got it immediately and excitedly told the class, "We were burdened by what we were carrying around just like Macbeth was burdened by the murder of King Duncan". As each student processed the explanation, their faces lit up with delighted surprise. Macbeth's feelings *and* actions made more sense to them, and they didn't have to listen to me pontificate for ten minutes. Win! I saved at least three minutes of class time overall, and my students appeared far more interested in the lesson.

Some of you likely recognize my example as constructivism…the theory of learning that posits students learn best when work is meaningful and relevant to them, and work becomes meaningful and relevant when they construct their own understanding through experience (Bada 66). And it totally was! This theory deeply resonated with me; as a student, I had always been impatient with explanation and preferred to learn by doing. I was thrilled to discover there was a name for my own preference and that scientists had studied it and created methodology. When I applied this framework to my class, I was pleased with the results. My students seemed happier, more engaged, and ultimately more successful. Their feedback to me – both informal and formal – shifted in a positive direction. Learning was more joyful because it was driven by a process of discovery. I felt like I was getting closer to being a "real" teacher…one who actually helps students find what's great in them and then nurtures that greatness.

There are trends in education just as there are trends in fashion, food, or art. In the 2000s, one of the trends was to be "student-centered". What "student-centered" meant varied wildly. Some people thought it meant, "Okay, the student comes first", while others thought it meant "Students need agency in the classroom". As my knowledge and understanding of educational practices deepened, I became convinced that student-centered meant both that student needs come first *and* that students need choice. Further, I observed that students were more successful – and happier – completing projects they chose. So choice became a critical element of what I offered: students could choose the genre in which they wrote, the topics they wrote about, and the kinds of projects they'd pursue. Additionally, students could choose the books they read. While this was arguably the best change for students – because they finally got to read what they liked for school – it was the hardest for me to figure out. Throughout my life, the focus in English class was the text all students presumably read, and I wasn't quite sure how to run a 75-minute class that didn't involve going over that shared text. However, I recognized that the time spent "going over" the book was the most boring part of my class, which was apparent by looking at the faces of my students. About 5 out of 18 were interested, while the rest stared into space. What a waste of time. Improving this situation was a priority for me, so I committed to figuring out how to offer reading choice.

The final frontier in my journey was to tackle student assessment and grading. While the feedback I got from students improved over time, that feedback also indicated I had failed to make my grading system clear. I had a hard time wrapping my head around this, as I felt like I spent so much time writing detailed comments on papers and going over expectations before papers were even due. Consequently, I experimented with writing rubrics, which I had learned about through various articles and books about writing. I reviewed models and ultimately wrote my own. Over a period of years, I refined the rubric until I had a total of five areas of competence. I rolled these out over the course of the year, adding a new skill when all students had mastered the three "base" skills. Then I set myself the task of understanding competency-based/performance-based assessment. Thanks to my school, which unwaveringly supported teachers who wanted to improve their practice, I again read deeply, went to conferences, and took classes. While I had always believed an English grade should be based on papers and projects rather than quizzes and tests, through my new competency-based assessment lens, I removed all extraneous assessment from the grade. I made sure there were plenty of opportunities for formative assessment, and, as had already been my practice, every paper could be rewritten for a completely new grade. Through a web browser extension called "Loom", I added video/audio explanations to my written feedback, which students really appreciated. Papers were not graded until students implemented the feedback given over several drafts. Finally, I involved students in the evaluation process. When it was time to grade the papers, I asked students to use the rubric to grade themselves. They had to explain where their work fell on the rubric and why. If the student's assessment and my assessment didn't align, I explained the steps the student could take to meet the rubric guidelines and invited them to rewrite. And here's what happened: my students thrived! Moving the locus of control from me to them in terms of assessment not only relieved their anxiety, but it also kindled intrinsic motivation, or meaning and relevance. They *wanted* to do well, they understood *how* to do well, so they tried harder. What was also great is that if they failed, they knew they could try again. The entire dynamic of how we "did school" shifted so that students were in charge. I loved it and so did they.

What I discovered as I grew into being an effective teacher is that joyful learning is meaningful, authentic, connected, and playful. The "joy" comes from the fact that the ways we learn best and the ways we experience happiness share many of the same qualities. These include the following:

- ◆ Meaning
- ◆ Autonomy
- ◆ Connection
- ◆ Mastery
- ◆ Positive emotions, like humor, enthusiasm, curiosity, gratitude, and optimism

Consider this typical day in English class:

Every student is absorbed in their work, whether it's writing, building an artwork, or discussing next steps in a project with a classmate. The air thrums with industry: keyboards click, scissors slice through paper, and Scotch tape unspools. Occasionally, a student races over to me and asks a breathless question. When I answer, the student's eyes light up and they say, "That's what I thought!", then hasten back to their work area to complete the task. Someone laughs and someone else joins in. "Mrs. Farley!" the laughing student calls, wanting to include me in the joke. One student finishes early and asks someone seated near them to read what was written or to look at what was made. The reviewer calls yet another student over, "OMG, Mathilda, check out what Chris just wrote! It's so good!" Four students stand up and crowd around Chris's laptop, straining to see Chris's remarkable sentences. Eventually, these four kids return to their laptops and furiously peck at their keyboards. When time is up, every student shares what they just created, and every student hears about the strengths their peers found in the work. Chris smiles and ducks his head in response to the positive feedback.

In this scene, the engagement is a result of work that the students have chosen and therefore find meaningful. They feel connected to one another and to me. They practice their skills through individualized challenges and celebrate each other's achievements. This is a classroom kids *want* to be in.

I wrote this book so I can share what I've learned and how you can apply the principles of joyful learning to your classroom.

Summary

- Effective teaching requires education and iteration.
- A student-centered perspective is a lens through which to view curriculum, instruction, and assessment.
- Learning that lasts and happiness share the traits of meaning, agency, mastery, connection, and positive emotions.
- Joyful learning is meaningful, authentic, connected, and playful.

Works Cited

Bada, Steve Olusegun. "Constructivism Learning Theory: A Paradigm for Teaching and Learning". *IOSR Journal of Research & Method in Education.* Vol 5, Issue 6, Version 1, pp 66–70, 2015. https://iosrjournals.org/iosr-jrme/papers/Vol-5%20Issue-6/Version-1/I05616670.pdf. Accessed 14 September 2022.

2

Joyful Relationships

The First Day

First impressions are powerful, so over time I've developed a first-day routine that signals to my students what to expect in the class while also asserting my prime directive as an instructor: help students identify their strengths and figure out how to use those strengths to enable growth of skills. I am not there to judge them, give them grades, or write a list of all they cannot do. It is important to me that students understand that the learning will be driven by them, and that I want to get to know them because this is how I can help them best.

Here is my agenda for the first day of class (with a class length of 75 minutes):

1   Introductions with a response to a question that would allow us to remember one another (i.e., "last movie you watched" or "last book you read" or "favorite food").
2   Show learning platform for class webpage.
3   Put kids into groups; assign each group an element of the class webpage (i.e., "homework policy" or "assessment") to learn; ask each team to present three salient points to the entire group.
4   Re-shuffle groups, ask teams to write rules for the class.
5   Establish rules as a large group.

DOI: 10.4324/9781003374909-2

6   I deliberately don't give a writing assignment in the first class. It's too anxiety-provoking. Instead, I give the kids art supplies – paper, markers, paper clips, string, pipe cleaners, tape, scissors, googly eyes, paper bags, leaves – and ask them to create an object that represents some aspect of their identity. Then, I ask each person to share their object. Everyone is expected to share.

Most of this agenda is self-explanatory, but I'll point out a few items:

◆ I didn't go over the class webpage with the kids because they could read it themselves and teach the rest of the class the parts they thought were important. Listening to me drone on was boring!

◆ I had the kids write the rules for the class, which I told them was based on their background knowledge of how classrooms run well and what they had just read on the class webpage. For example, did knowing that they will evaluate themselves change any of the rules[1] for class conduct?

◆ Artmaking can be anxiety-provoking, but because it was art in an English class, the kids saw that I wasn't evaluating them; I was truly just interested in learning about them as they learned about each other. Additionally, this activity set the tone that the primary mode of learning in my class was doing…experiences rather than memorization.

The reason that I know my first day agenda works is because of student feedback: they told me in their writing, in their formal evaluations of me, and in their informal chit-chat later in the year.

In recent years, teacher Instagram has documented and celebrated the creation of warm, inviting spaces for learning. While I don't have great decorating skills, I am mindful of the furniture in the room and how it can be arranged to meet my goal of creating a joyful, connected community. As a middle school teacher, I prefer one large table that all students fit comfortably around, but more often than not find myself shoving a number of 6-foot rectangular tables together to get a similar effect. I sit at the same big table as the students while we chat, but I walk around the table as students work. Seats are unassigned, which is intended to create a more casual, friendly atmosphere. Most of the time, students work better seated near their friends than away from them: they can ask each other questions, talk about the books or stories, and work on projects together. And, having agency in this arena contributes to student satisfaction.

This first day routine isn't particularly innovative, but I hope it captures the spirit with which the students and I work, which is with curiosity, compassion, and a sense of delight in discovering what is awesome about each other. Please note that my goal on the first day is not to "scare" kids or impress upon them how serious or hard my class is. In fact, it is quite the opposite. I want to convey that English class is a safe space to chillax and have fun with ideas.

The First Month

The first month of school is the time to create routines, ways of being, and understandings in the classroom that you'll build upon later. I didn't think of this concept on my own: I learned it from people way smarter than me. When I first started as a teacher, I used the first month to jam in as many assignments as possible, in part so I could understand each child's strengths and in part so I would have grades in my gradebook for midterm reporting. These are bad reasons to assess! You should only formally assess when students have developed mastery of the target skills, which you know by doing a ton of *informal, non-graded* assessments. So I changed my practice, and the result was students were calmer because they knew what was expected, more focused when it was time to work, and more invested in the routines because they helped develop them.

The most important understandings to build are around the learning targets. For example, the main learning targets in my class were about writing, which I broke down into "big idea", "specific details", and "mechanics". Consequently, I'd use the first four weeks of school to engage in non-graded activities that built student understanding of big idea, specific details, and mechanics. My path to doing so looked like this:

1   I read a story to the class…sometimes a very simple story, like Mo Willem's *The Pigeon Finds a Hot Dog*, and sometimes a more complicated story, like Neil Gaiman's "Murder Mystery".
2   I asked students to identify the big idea of the story.
3   Students worked together to generate a list of big ideas from the story.
4   Before the next class, I'd take the big ideas the students generated and put them onto mailing labels.
5   As students entered the room, I handed them a sticky label with a big idea on it, which they usually affixed to their shirt.

6   I put a collection of objects on the table, like stuffed animals, small toys, flowers I found outside, buttons, and candy.

7   I asked students to select an object from the table, then write four to five sentences about the object, *incorporating the big idea on their label*. So, for example, students may have had a label with the big idea of LONGING and they'd selected a stuffed elephant as their object. Their sentences might describe how the elephant really longed for a friend, or an adventure, or to learn how to roller skate.

For students to be successful, it's crucial for them to understand what is expected *and* how to do it. Through the steps outlined above, students constructed their own understanding of big ideas, how they show up in what we read, and how they can be used in their writing, and the pattern was repeated for other learning targets. This work was not graded, but I read it and provided feedback. Often, I'd ask everyone to share what they wrote in class and then I'd point out the strengths in every single student's writing. In this way, you build students' confidence, sense of competence, and your relationship with them, as I demonstrated that my job was to identify what worked rather than what didn't. If students veered off target, I'd simply redirect or ask gentle questions about what the student's intention was. Sidebar: it's really valuable to ask students about their intentions rather than assuming you know. Hearing a student's reasoning about why they made a particular choice in their writing is illuminating, as often you discover another way of understanding that is delightful and doesn't require your correction. At the end of the first month, students had enough practice with the requirements of the learning targets to take on a project or paper that would be graded.

As mentioned, I also used the first month of school to establish routines and ways of being. In my "learn through doing" model, students learned how to access and submit their assignments on Google Classroom by doing it, which meant I didn't spend class time explaining a theory. Instead, when it was relevant, I'd show students what to do and then they'd immediately apply that routine. When it was time to have a discussion about a work we'd read together, I'd demonstrate the expectation of cordial conversations and then ask students to engage in a discussion using those conventions. For example, after one student spoke, another student could respond by saying, "I agree with Vivek, and I'd like to add…" or perhaps, "To build on what Vivek said…". While the sentence starters were stilted at first, eventually they were adopted as a normal standard of discussion.

By deliberately using our time together in this way, I was also building relationships with my students. You may have wondered why this chapter is titled "Joyful Relationships" when I haven't written much about relationships at all. The reason is that the activities and routines I've described also served to build my relationships with the students. As I observed how students interacted with (or failed to interact with) one another, as I saw how they took on the small, in-class assignments, and as I read their writing, I grew to know them a little better. And when I refrained from constant correction and grading, the kids started to feel more comfortable. Finally, when I mentioned – both publicly and privately – what I saw them doing well, they knew I was on their side. All of this built trust, safety, and, eventually, a willingness to take risks.

To help illustrate my point here, I'll give an example of what *not* to do. In my first year of teaching, I struggled to balance my pedagogical goals with the needs of the students to talk about all the other topics on their minds, like sports, friendships, and what was on the menu for lunch. One day midway through the year, I bribed a particularly rambunctious class by promising that if they'd settle into a grammar lesson, I'd let them ask me any questions they liked afterwards. Tragic rookie mistake. Not only is it a ridiculously bad idea to run an "ask me anything" session with kids, but I also had not realized the extent to which I had fostered animosity among some of my students with my grading, feedback, and general ignorance about how to develop relationships. When it was question time, a male student I'll call Rufus asked me if I had ever had an abortion. I was shocked, the class erupted, and all I could think to do was say, "that's not an appropriate question". Later, shaken and a bit righteous, I spoke to the dean, who advised me to call the student's parents. I did. But when Rufus's mom spoke to her 12-year-old son, he shared how I had spent half a school year calling him out, embarrassing him, and making him feel that I didn't like or value him. That mom called my principal and explained her son's point of view, which of course the principal shared with me. I was flabbergasted that Rufus felt so unhappy in my class, as he was a cheerful, cheeky 7th grader who always had a smile on his face. However, I had dimmed Rufus's sparkle, and when he saw an opportunity to make a joke at my expense, he took it.

What happened, I eventually realized, was that Rufus was new to the school and struggled a bit with fluency and comprehension in reading and writing. Meanwhile, I hadn't yet learned how to differentiate or individualize instruction. What I asked Rufus to do in class was well beyond what I should have been asking any 7th grader to do, so his grades were not stellar. Rufus hadn't earned a mark lower than an "A" before, and the grades had a significantly negative impact on his identity and confidence. To make matters worse, without realizing it, I had also interacted with him in ways that made him feel like all I saw were his deficits. My feedback to him was almost entirely negative or about what he lacked, because at that time I lacked the skill of offering feedback that fosters growth.

I had failed in kindness, in compassion, and in the fundamental premise of teaching: that building a positive, constructive relationship with a student is the most effective way to teach them. While Rufus's abortion question was rude, *my actions generated his negative feelings about me.*

Rufus's mom wanted me to meet with her son to make sure he knew that I cared about him. So, with the principal and Rufus's mom present, I apologized to Rufus for not acknowledging all that he did well, explained that I cared about his progress, and asked if we could start again. While I can't say I won over Rufus, we were able to move forward with a better understanding.

As an example of what I learned about joyful relationships, I offer my student Lulu. Sharp, witty, independent, and worldly, having Lulu in class was like hanging out with Dorothy Parker. She'd look up from editing a playlist to toss out incisive yet warm and supportive analyses of her classmates' written work. I appreciated that she noticed other's excellence and remarked upon it with delicacy and care. She wasn't as loving with herself: in her own eyes, her work was never good enough. However, she was a gifted writer who came up with dozens of ideas that she wrote in a flurry of activity. I met with her to show her all the ways in which her writing was extraordinary: the word choice, the complexity of her characters, the structure matched to the type of story. By this time in my English class, students chose what they read and what they wrote, which happily aligned with Lulu's desire to not be told what to do or think. When Lulu grew weary of the stimulation of the class – the noise and clamor of kids writing and chatting – she'd go outside to sit quietly and get on with her work. When she was stuck on a plot point, she asked me what I would do. She almost always rejected my ideas, but talking it out helped her get writing again. If Lulu had been in my class in my first years of teaching, I wouldn't have been an effective teacher for her: she would have shut down due to the monotony of my instruction. The key to success with her was respect; I respected her autonomy, and she respected me for not trying to control her. I figured all of this out by observing her actions and pauses, identifying her strengths, and being her number one cheerleader. One way I was her cheerleader is that I emailed her early in the year, cc-ing her parents, to tell her that I thought she was a talented writer and that I was impressed with the skill she demonstrated in her stories. I knew I was a successful teacher for Lulu because I saw her progress, and both Lulu and her parents told me that I made a difference for her.

What I'm writing about joyful relationships, then, comes from direct experience of what happens when you don't pay attention and what happens when you do. I recognize now that if I had built a more positive and proactive relationship with Rufus, he wouldn't have asked me that question about abortion; indeed, if he truly felt that I cared about him, he wouldn't have wanted to embarrass me. Once I prioritized joyful relationships, I never had a problem like the abortion question again.

Below is a quick rundown of tips for building joyful relationships.

◆ Get to know your students. I recognize this seems self-evident, but it's worth repeating because it's so important. Have them write about themselves in fun ways (i.e., put themselves at the center of a mystery in their house, like "the mystery of my brother's missing striped sock"), answer questions about themselves, and create projects that highlight their identities. One math teacher I know asks kids their birthdays and then says, "Oh, you're a prime number" or "Hey! You're divisible by 3".

◆ For students to feel safe enough to show themselves to you, you have to create a welcoming environment that actively demonstrates inclusivity. As an English teacher, this has meant allowing kids to read all kinds of stories showcasing a spectrum of identities, rather than the heteronormative, white, middle-class identity usually represented in "literature". One of my students gave an end of year speech to the entire school in which she mentioned that discovering a gay character in a story assigned for my class made her feel seen. I also allow students to choose their own reading material and to write about what appeals to them. This creates a safe space, as each child can use content that engages them as a vehicle for growth.

◆ Identify each child's strengths and sing them a song of their excellence instead of their deficits. Let them know you see them and value their contributions. An easy way to do this is have the kids write four to five sentences to a prompt. Ask every student to share their writing (they will grumble at first and ask if they can *not* share…ask them to just read one sentence instead, and usually they'll agree). Sometimes a simple "thanks for sharing" is all you need to say, but you can also comment on what was unique about what was read. You might say something like, "I appreciate your use of the word 'intractable', Sam, as it suited the situation you described".

A history teacher I know keeps track of who she's called on each class so she can: (1) Make sure everyone has a chance to speak; and (2) Ensure that she provides encouragement and support to each student.

A math teacher I know knocks on students' desks in celebration when they've completed the steps of a problem. It's a simple yet totally affirming tool.

◆ Kindling positive emotions has a significant impact on relationships, because self-regulation increases in the presence of positive emotions (Baumeister et al.; Tice et al.). In other words, when kids come to your class strained from tamping down their impulses all day, they are not in a great frame of mind to learn or to connect with others. However, research has shown that positive emotions like humor, curiosity, enthusiasm, and gratitude bolster people's ability to self-regulate after their emotional equilibrium has been depleted (Baumeister et al.; Tice et al.). Therefore, I like to use my framing activities to also boost positive emotions. I accomplish this by thinking about what makes my students laugh, what elicits surprise or astonishment, and what piques their curiosity. In Chapter 6, I explain a few framing activities I've used that also kindle positive emotions.

◆ One of the elements of happiness is feeling as though you have agency in your life (Deci and Ryan 14–15). Agency in turn creates meaning. Accordingly, I've tried to remove all the barriers to agency that exist in a traditional classroom. For example, my students sit where they like and go to the bathroom without asking. I let them work with their friends and eat if they're hungry. And, most importantly, I provide agency in curricular matters, which I'll explain further in the next chapter. An emphasis on autonomy contributes to joyful relationships because it is a demonstration of respect.

◆ Joyful relationships aren't just between you and your students; you should also consider how to build relationships *among* your students. By this I mean it's important to remember that your class is not your opportunity to be on stage and pontificate about your favorite subtopics, like why the Oxford comma is the only proper way to punctuate a series of three items. Rather, your classroom should be the place where students can discover what interests them about the subject you teach and, most importantly, learn from each other. My favorite way to do this is having them get to know each other through their writing and the little in-class projects I have them do. As I said above, any time they write or create, I ask the students to share, and then I point out what I appreciated or enjoyed about what was shared. After a few weeks, students get in on the act of indicating what they appreciate about other's work. By December, the students are aware of each other's special abilities and as a result will say, "Alicia is so good at characters. I'm going to ask her what she thinks about the characters in my story". I remember one student in particular, Nick, who really knew the punctuation rules. By the end of the year, he was reading the stories of almost everyone in class and giving them pointers on their grammar. It made him feel great and it helped the other kids, who saw Nick as an invaluable expert. Encouraging your students to work with and learn from each other creates an authentic, joyous community.

◆ When you give feedback, don't make a long list of all the "areas for improvement", as this is discouraging and kids may take this feedback as a sign you don't like them. Instead, focus on one or two growth areas at a time. Humans don't get good at stuff by trying to improve everything all at once; rather, we improve when we practice a few specific skills, over and over. When kids can actually see the improvement, it builds their confidence and sense of competence.

◆ Create time to learn about your students – and for them to get to know each other – through play. Play is a natural and excellent way for students to learn. It's also an effective way for you to understand more about each person…do they prefer logic and reasoning or a more flexible, creative approach? Can they strategize? Can they gracefully accept loss? Do they collaborate? Work alone? Do they like to make up their own rules? Use this information to craft activities and assignments.

Creating a foundation of joyful relationships is the only way you can actually teach your students anything; without that base of trust and care, all your students will learn is how to make it *look* like they're working during your class.

I'll offer more detail about choice, challenge, and play in the following chapters.

Summary

◆ Use the first day to establish the tone of the class, which is one of community and agency.
◆ Use the first month to teach the language of the learning targets so that students feel connected to the methods of evaluation and understand the meaning and relevance of the work they'll do.
◆ Let students know what their strengths are in your discipline.
◆ Consider how to start every class with positive emotions, which helps students regulate their own behavior and creates a joyful environment for learning.
◆ Use play to build a sense of connection among students and to learn how students function best in the classroom.

Note

1 In case you are curious, the rules the kids wrote usually included "respect everyone's opinion"; "respect other people's stuff"; and "do your work".

Works Cited

Baumeister, R. F., Vohs, K. D. and Tice, D. M. "The Strength Model of Self-Control". *Current Directions in Psychological Science*. Vol 16, Issue 6, pp 351–355, 2007.

Deci, Edward L. and Ryan, Richard M. "Facilitating Optimal Motivation and Psychological Well-Being Across Life's Domains". *Canadian Psychology*. Vol 49, Issue 1, pp 14–23, 2008.

Gaiman, Neil. "Murder Mystery". *Smoke and Mirrors: Short Fictions and Illusions*. Avon Books, 1998.

Tice Dianne, M., Baumeister, Roy F., Shmueli, Dikla and Muraven, Mark. "Restoring the Self: Positive Affect Helps Improve Self-Regulation Following Ego Depletion". *Journal of Experimental Social Psychology*, Vol 43, Issue 3, pp 379–384, 2007, ISSN 0022-1031.

Willems, Mo. *The Pigeon Finds a Hot Dog*. Hyperion, 2004.

3

Joyful Curriculum

Back in Chapter 1, I mentioned that the term "student-centered" became an educational trend in the 2000s. It had probably been percolating long before then – John Dewey was "student-centered" (teachthought.com) – but it broke through the private, independent-school bubble in which I operated some-time around…2003? I was taken by the terminology, as it immediately just *sounded* right. Yeah! Student-centered! That's how school *should* be. I completely bought it. But then I had to figure out what it meant for my teaching.

Around this time, in my quest to make my class more student-centered, I took an online Understanding by Design class. The two significant contributions of that class to my pedagogical practice were essential questions and backwards planning.

Essential Questions

For those who may be unfamiliar, essential questions are a series of scaled questions that focus the scope of learning in the classroom. If you want a proper education about essential questions, then I recommend Grant Wiggins and Jay McTighe's book, *Understanding by Design*. Here, I'll share my use of essential questions as a way to drive the curriculum and make my class more student-centered.

As I considered how I might use an essential question with my own class, I thought about what my students tended to be interested in as we read and

DOI: 10.4324/9781003374909-3

wrote our way through the year. The kinds of stories that seemed to get the best responses (by which I mean, bright, shining eyes, enthusiastic contributions, excited swapping of tall tales) were ones that involved monsters, competition, and chaos: "Monster" by Kelly Link; "To Scratch, Claw, Or Grope Clumsily Or Frantically" by Roxane Gay; or "Angel" by Darryl "DMC" McDaniels. Additionally, I observed in my students a striving for meaning… they had a sweet, earnest desire to understand themselves and their places in the world. So, the essential question I wrote to organize our inquiries in 8th grade English class was:

In the face of chaos, what makes life worth living?

For me, this question captured the pathos and yearning I saw in students' writing. At first, I used this question in the following ways:

1 When I chose books for the curriculum, I considered whether the books had anything to say about what makes life worth living.
2 I presented the essential question at the beginning of the year and explained that the question would organize our thinking and discussions.
3 At the end of every book, I'd bring up the essential question and have students think and write about what the book revealed about the question.
4 For the end of year summative assessment, students wrote about this question in some form.

Eventually, I shifted gear into this more specific and evocative question:

In the face of monsters, madness, and mayhem, what makes life worth living?

Even when students selected their own books, this question worked because it served as the glue that bound the readers together. The kids liked hearing about how monsters, madness, or mayhem showed up in books about friendship, basketball, or living up to parents' expectations. The question became the theme of the class and allowed students to explore their existential selves. In addition, the essential question provided a focus for assignments and projects.

For essential questions to be useful to you and to the students, they need to be high-level – by which I mean they need to encourage students to tap into higher order thinking – and broad enough to apply to lots of situations.

I mention this because I've seen curricula that use reductive essential questions, like, "What are the qualities of paper?" Maybe I'm exaggerating with that one, but my point is the essential question should be fun to think about and have many possible answers.

Some teachers I've met write essential questions that guide each unit and each day. I tried that for a while, but once I fully expanded reading and writing choices, I abandoned the practice. Not only were my questions distracting the kids from asking their own, but I also struggled to write so many questions that I thought were truly excellent.

When you first start teaching or working with a particular age group, you obviously don't have the benefit of knowing hundreds of students who help you home in on an interesting question to spend the year exploring. In these scenarios, what you do instead is consider what it is you want students to *know* and be *able to do* by the end of the school year. Then, you think about how students can best master both the content and the skills…what are the steps on the way to mastery? Finally, you ask a question that guides students to take the cognitive steps that will lead them to understanding. In my case, I wanted students to identify big ideas in stories that they could learn from and apply to their own lives. The steps one must take to master big ideas include reading, processing, and reflecting. Therefore, the essential question I ended up with – *in the face of monsters, madness, and mayhem, what makes life worth living?* – required students to:

- ◆ Read the story…which means they knew the basic plot and characters.
- ◆ Process the story…which means they could identify the monsters, madness, or mayhem contained therein.
- ◆ Reflect on the story…which means they could develop an understanding of what made life worth living for the characters as well as themselves.

A strong essential question for a social studies class might be about the significance of water or what creates culture, while in science class students might be intrigued by a question about the nature of the universe.

Backwards Planning

The other critical concept that I learned from my Understanding by Design class was backwards planning. It's such an elegant idea that you can trick yourself into believing you already thought of it. But I hadn't. Of course,

I knew what I wanted to accomplish by year's end, but I often fell short of my lofty goals. The process of backwards planning gave me a logical structure for achieving my desired learning outcomes. Again, for a full explanation, I refer you to Grant Wiggins' and Jay McTighe's book.

My simplistic understanding of backwards planning was this:

1   Identify a learning outcome.
2   Consider the steps required to reach that outcome.
3   Design the unit/project/lessons that build to the desired outcome.

Yeah, I know…it's not mind-blowing, as the process is exactly like it sounds: planning backwards. But for some reason, it just resonated with me and I thought it was *genius*. This is likely because I lacked a foundation in pedagogical theories; in fact, one of my co-teachers later told me that she had learned the Understanding by Design principles in her University of Pennsylvania teacher training program! The fact that someone had laid out a methodology for learning that made so much sense delighted me, and I eagerly applied this process to my curriculum.

Before I instituted backwards planning, my learning outcomes were broad and pretty sketchy, like, "develop strong critical thinking". The reason this is a sketchy goal is because it lacks specificity and the kids had no idea what it meant, so I couldn't fairly assess it. As far as they were concerned, yes, they absolutely had strong critical thinking! After all, they knew when they didn't like a book or thought what someone said was stupid. Bam. Critical thinking.

Backwards planning is a student-centered process because it puts what students *know* and *can do* at the center of curriculum design. After I learned about backwards planning, I sharpened my learning outcomes, which also shifted what and how I taught. Consequently, lessons, assignments, and projects became more focused on what students were actually interested in and developed their skills such that, by the end of the year, every single student reliably could, for example, "Write a story or essay with a big idea in mind".

I'll write more about learning targets in the next chapter, but once you've crafted clear, specific learning targets, backwards planning is a breeze!

Choice

Giving students choices in the classroom is another one of those concepts that has been around for a long time, but it didn't really enter my consciousness as a solid, research-based practice until I was well into my teaching career. Most of my own models for learning had required me to do whatever the teacher told me, and I was good at that, so I didn't have a schema for student choice.

However, as I sought to be more student-centered and to make English a joyful class, I experimented with choice. As a psychology undergraduate I had been exposed to theories by Maslow and others that indicated agency increases intrinsic motivation. It made a lot of sense to me when I considered my own experience and felt the theory's truth. Later, as I read more deeply about learning theory and then took a positive psychology class, I again encountered research that indicates humans invest more in their work when they choose it or feel a sense of agency in it (Deci and Ryan 14).

My unsophisticated understanding about how choice interacts with learning is as follows:

- Humans are geared to prefer activities that we choose for ourselves.
- Even if we have to choose between two unpleasant activities, we'll perceive the chosen activity as less unpleasant than the alternative, *because we chose it.*
- Choices give humans a sense of agency, which is motivating.
- Offering students choice allows them to play to their strengths.
- Giving students choice shows that you respect their preferences and proclivities, which helps to create safe, trusting, and respectful relationships.

These understandings, fortunately, matched my own experiences in the classroom, so I resolved to consistently give students a choice in assignments. My first makeovers were of the big projects or papers I assigned each term. Instead of assigning an essay, I gave students three choices of writing genres: an essay, a fictional story, or a personal narrative. Eventually I removed this three-choice framework to allow students to write in whatever format they liked. Additionally, I took note of topics that came up in conversations and crafted assignments based on those student-generated topics. Then I turned my attention to providing choices in the daily lessons and activities. Since the students spent a good deal of class time practicing writing, I made sure there were choices within those smaller practice sessions.

Around this same time, I researched Lucy Calkin's reading workshop model (readingandwritingproject.org).[1] The part of her program that captured my attention was the idea that kids could select their own reading material. I just wasn't sure how to make it happen in middle school. Again, I had no schema for reading choice. In my little world, English class had always meant the teacher picked the books. The problem, I knew, was that every kid wasn't like me! Administrator types may tell you that if you love your subject, the kids will love it, too. I'm here to say that this logic is a bit flawed. Case in point: even though I was enchanted by *Night Circus* by Erin Morgenstern, I could not convince Ethan – a wry, outdoorsy intellectual – that it was a great read. He was not buying it. And when people don't like books, they don't read them. Ask any English teacher how many times they've been frustrated by a classroom full of kids who clearly haven't completed the reading assignment, and they'll tell you it's been at least 17 million times. This means that discussions about the book were a complete waste…how can a student contribute and learn from a conversation when they don't know what their peers are talking about? I was done with trying to cajole students to read my great book picks for the following reasons:

1   It wasn't student-centered. *I was selecting the books.*
2   I wanted students to develop a love for reading. Love flourishes in the presence of choice.
3   I wanted to build affirming relationships with students, which also meant I had to affirm and encourage their understanding of what they liked.

Ultimately, I had to shift how I thought of "literature" time in class. Reading didn't have to be about a group of students and a teacher gathering in a room together to "discuss" elements of the book. Instead, it could be about students using a book they chose for themselves to explore setting, plot, characters, and theme *on their own*. This was a major realization, as class discussion was pretty much how time was spent in secondary English classes. Switching the model felt like a significant innovation.

Another factor that spurred my progress in this area was that, for years, I had set aside one to two times per year when students could select what I called a "free read"…a book of their choice. This was consistently a positive and popular unit for the students. I adapted the protocols of the free read units to suit my updated learning goals.

My next move was to create a long list of suggested books, which I presented at the beginning of the year and told the students they could pick from. However, I wasn't at all disciplined about this list. The first time someone asked me if they could read a book they already had at home that wasn't on the list, I said yes. I was thrilled. Forget the list![2] Ultimately, I diverged from the Reader's Workshop model because I didn't mind when students wanted to read a book that maybe was a little too hard or too easy for them. They should be the boss of that rather than me. Not incidentally, this was another building block in my relationship with students: they saw that I trusted them to find what was right and that I really just wanted them to enjoy what they read. Finally and most significantly, allowing students choice of reading material is an inclusive practice, as students seek stories that speak to their lives and experience. Not every 8th grader is keen to understand the history of the Iranian Cultural Revolution – even when it's presented in comics form – but one kid whose family happened to be from Iran was pretty into it, and when she chose to read *Persepolis*, she was able to dive in to the elements that interested her without hearing how boring Marjane's life was from some other kid who didn't want to read a book with a female protagonist.

There were other ways I offered choice, such as having students vote at the beginning of the year whether they wanted to take vocabulary quizzes, asking them about genres of writing they wanted to explore, and, eventually, allowing complete freedom around projects. As long as the work the students engaged in met the learning targets, how we got there didn't matter. However, by the time I opened up this much choice, I was *super clear* about my learning targets. Having that framework enabled me to provide expansive choices.

The main reason offering choices is such a compelling practice is because it automatically makes the work more meaningful and relevant to the students. In the classroom, the result is that students experience intrinsic motivation to perform the various tasks that build their skills. Improving at a skill like writing requires a ton of practice, which can be tedious. But when students are allowed to write about topics they've chosen, in styles they've chosen, the tedium diminishes. When students get to write a story that they've conceived of from start to finish, they have fun. My student Judah loved superhero movies and comics. Every single project he wrote in 8th grade was about the same superhero, and he was the happiest, most engaged, and motivated writer. When students were in the thick of their projects, he'd swing by my office a few times a day to share an idea he'd just had for a character or a plot twist. He was thinking about his story all the time. Similarly, when students can select their own reading material, they want to read and are motivated to learn from their books. In short, choice is the vehicle for meaning, relevance, *and* joy.

Challenge

One of the reasons I love giving students choice is because doing so means that they simultaneously opt in to appropriate challenges. An "appropriate challenge" is in what's called the zone of proximal development (McLeod), which is that delicate space between work that is either too hard or too easy. When work is too easy, of course, we get bored, while we give up when work is too hard. Finding the zone of proximal development is a real win for students because it keeps them engaged and motivated.[3]

When a new school year begins, I don't focus on figuring out appropriate challenges right away. Instead, I focus on helping each student understand their strengths and offer a variety of modes of working to see which modes suit them best (i.e., group vs. independent work; stories vs. essays vs. narratives). Once we've established this baseline, we can tinker with appropriate challenges through the choices students make about the work they do. An easy way to illustrate this is through reading choices. I always start the year with a short story that everyone reads, and I observe how students respond to the story. Are they confused by the plot or do they apprehend it immediately? Do they understand the motivations and nuances of the characters? Are they able to establish meaningful takeaways from the story, or do they strain to make sense of it? Then, when it's time to select reading material, I make a list of the books each student selects. If I don't know the title, I'll ask a few questions…what genre is it? Have they read anything like this book before? Where did they hear about it?

Within my 8th grade cohort, students self-selected books ranging from relatively difficult, like Bram Stoker's *Dracula*, to relatively easy, like Kathi Appelt's *The Underneath*. These choices provided me with significant information about the readers in my class. For example, when a student selected a book I suspected they already read – like *The Underneath*, which is often assigned in upper elementary – it revealed that the student was more comfortable with books that were smooth, easy reading. The reading zone of proximal development for this student would be another "upper elementary" book, like *Clean Getaway* by Nic Stone. Similarly, when a student selected *Dracula*, it told me that they wanted a challenge, as the language of Stoker's 1897 work is hard to understand for 14-year-olds in the year 2022. An appropriate challenge for this student might be a book like *Neverwhere* by Neil Gaiman.

This same cycle of observation and selection was true for writing, as well. Because students had choice in their writing assignments, I observed the challenges they took on willingly and guided them to increase the challenge in order to progress in the skill.

Challenge in the curriculum fosters meaning, relevance, and joy. For these reasons, it is incredibly valuable. However, I'm not into forcing students to accept challenges they aren't ready for or withholding challenges students desire. It's up to each student to determine the level at which they want to work. The analogy I like to make here is to exercise: no trainer or coach can force me to do one more push up or deadlift. Completing one more deadlift is entirely my decision, which I make based on my desire to strain beyond my perceived limit or be satisfied with what I've accomplished so far. The same is true for student learning: I can't make a child read a book. In order for reading to happen, they have to want to read then commit themselves to the act of reading. I recognize that this stance can be interpreted as lacking rigor. However, my experience is that rigor comes from within each individual. I set the learning targets for the class, but the progress each student makes toward mastery of that target is a result of their will to learn.

As a teacher, my role is to create the conditions in which students want to push themselves. That's why I am interested in play.

Play

My favorite teachers when I was growing up were the ones who played with us…who were dedicated to making learning fun and engaging by designing activities that spoke to our particular stage of development. For example, my 8th grade year in history was focused on learning American history content and then playing a game with it. The game itself was simple: throwing a crumpled up piece of paper into a trash can. But you could only throw the paper ball into the trash can if you earned the shot through demonstrating knowledge or a skill. I was a terrible shot, but I loved the game and so did my classmates. We were excited to learn the most facts about the Louisiana Purchase because it meant our team could earn more shots and points. That teacher tapped into our adolescent love of relatively skill-less competition. So when I became a teacher myself, I wanted to spread joy through playful instruction.

At first, I struggled. I thought it playful and fun to put kids' names in the vocabulary quizzes and grammar exercises. It turns out that worksheets and memorization aren't fun just because your name might be included! Then I thought, okay, it's fun to act out plays, so we'll put on a play. At the time, every grade in my school was required to teach one Shakespeare play. Ugh… what a nightmare! Not only did I have no talent for directing, staging, or *any aspect* of play production, but the time investment required to help all my students understand Shakespeare was enormous and only a handful of kids were truly interested. I moved on to simulations, like mock town halls or debates, with students representing the various sides of issues presented in books. This was too much like acting, so it was a failure. Model United Nations and mock trial competitions offered a model for potential play, but I just couldn't get it right in English class.

My big break in successful use of play in the classroom came when I read about constructivism and how students are more engaged when they construct their own understanding. Aha! Combining play with a construction of understanding was my way in. I started small, with framing activities, which take about ten minutes and set up students for what's going to happen in class that day. For example, when the writing lesson was about observation, I'd enlist my teacher friends to burst into my classroom shouting at one another to create a highly dramatic, absorbing scene. The teachers would barge in – ostensibly to pick up materials left in the room – while arguing about how one teacher took the other's parking space. They'd stop and apologize to me for interrupting, then begin arguing again. It lasted no longer than two or three minutes. When the teachers left, I'd say, *wow, that's quite a scene! Let's capture it. Write down everything you can remember from what just happened.* I'd give the students a few minutes to write, then they'd share. I'd ask questions until students figured out that the scene was faked and that I had arranged it so they could observe and record it. Then we'd move into the heart of the lesson about how writers observe details in real life that they can use in their stories. Students loved these demonstrations as the novelty of the interruption delighted them, and then they got to use the drama in their work! Lessons about writing instructions or "how-tos" started with kids getting stickers as they walked into the classroom with directions on them like, "Hop on one foot, pat your belly, then touch the floor" or "Pretend that you're sick and healthy to laugh maniacally. Rush onto the balcony to brush your teeth". Each student got a different set of directions and they were asked to enact the instructions all at the same time, so while one person was hopping on one foot, another was doing jumping jacks, and yet another was trying to laugh maniacally. Once all instructions were followed, the students had to determine which directions were clearest. This activity created joy through connection and play while also demonstrating the nuances in writing that support clarity.

To expand play I tapped into my students' interests. One year the students loved murder mysteries, so I created a murder mystery for them to solve, using the principal as the "victim" and planting clues around the school. Another group liked adventure stories, so I had them generate adventures for their peers. One team of students even secured the help of a teacher to transport kids from one end of campus to another on the school's golf cart for their adventure! Our play connected to a project they'd take on, such as writing their own murder mysteries or adventure stories. And always, there was choice; maybe 97% of the students liked a murder mystery, but for a few this genre was just too scary, so those kids would write another story of their choice. The projects connected students to one another, gave meaning to their work, and generated positive emotions.

In sum, for me, play meant taking a *playful approach*[4] to all the work of the class, which, of course, was building skills in writing and reading. It's worth noting that thinking of new modes of play made my own work as a teacher fresh; indeed, this thinking work motivated and inspired me. I loved figuring out what each student enjoyed and planning playful activities that engaged them: this was truly student-centered teaching. Each class, I couldn't wait to see their expressions when I rolled out the day's lesson. And I think my students were also excited to see what was on offer that day. English class can't be *all* murder mysteries, of course, but you can infuse all activities with a playful spirit. I visited a cool math class once, in which students were told they ran a gift wrap company and needed to figure out how much paper to put on each roll to create an average of five wrapped gifts per roll of paper. I've also heard of science classes that were year-long games of detection.

Individualize Instruction

"Differentiation" is another one of those words that's been in the educational lexicon for ages. At one time, differentiation seemed like the catch-all solution for traditionally thorny issues, like tracking, failing students, and "gifted" students. If you just differentiate, the thinking went, every student's needs would be met!

My math teacher friends, though, warned me that differentiation is nearly impossible in their classes. Their experience indicates that the gaps in skills between groups of students are just too vast to bridge with differentiation. Okay. I respect that. I don't know enough about teaching math to challenge this notion, but I do know it can be disheartening for kids to be placed in "ability" groups so I wish there were an alternative.

For other subjects, I'm convinced we can serve student needs by individualizing instruction. My conviction surely arises from the fact that I've always taught English, which, because it requires creativity, is a subject that lends itself to idiosyncrasy. Here's what I mean: let's say I give all students the same assignment of writing an adventure. Some of my students might jam that story out in an hour, while others struggle with each sentence and it takes days to craft a work of which they're proud. Still other students may write the beginning and middle of the story with ease, but they are frustrated by the lack of a proper ending. I individualize instruction by giving each writer whatever they need:

◆ Lots of scaffolding and sentence-by-sentence support for those who struggle.
◆ A brainstorm session with those who just can't nail their ending.
◆ Adding a character, rethinking the opening, or layering in more vivid descriptions of action and setting for those who wrote their story in an hour.

Individualizing instruction is also how you introduce appropriate challenges for each student. While the nature of English work easily allows for this kind of individualization, I think the same is true of other disciplines, as well. For example, the study of history and science allow for tailored projects. Dance, art, and music have long been differentiated because the level of mastery each person attains is varied. In each of these classrooms, the teacher's role is to provide what's needed by individual students, which is the hallmark of student-centered instruction. Individualizing instruction also serves to make the work more joyful because it has more meaning and relevance. Teachers know that when kids are bored, they tune out. But when you offer challenges that capitalize on a student's strengths, the work is far more engaging.

I recognize there are foundational skills all students need to master and individualizing that instruction may be impossible…like, for example, knowing the steps in the scientific method or memorizing a bunch of facts. As a middle school teacher, I didn't have to give students facts to memorize. Third-grade math teachers don't have that luxury. But once students move into applying their knowledge and skills, instruction *can* and *should* be individualized.

Lastly, to be clear, I'm not using "individualizing instruction" as a euphemism for tracking or ability grouping. Rather, I use the term to mean "provide each learner what they need in order to progress".

Student-centered learning is joyful learning and is constructed with these tools[5]:

- ◆ Essential questions
- ◆ Backwards planning
- ◆ Choice
- ◆ Challenge
- ◆ Play
- ◆ Individualized Instruction

In the next two chapters, I'll focus on the end products of student-centered learning, assessment and grading.

Summary

- ◆ Essential questions and backwards planning narrow the scope of the curriculum, which in turn helps students make measurable progress.
- ◆ The constructs of choice, challenge, and play prioritize students' preferences and strengths.

- ◆ Choice, challenge, and play in turn foster meaning, mastery, and positive emotions.
- ◆ Individualized instruction creates appropriate challenge, which makes the work relevant and engaging.
- ◆ When students experience autonomy, meaning, connection, mastery, and positive emotions, they want to be in class.

Notes

1 As I write this in 2022, I acknowledge that the Reader's Workshop model has detractors, especially for emerging readers. And, in response to the criticism, Lucy Calkins has rewritten her program (Goldstein www. nytimes.com).

2 If I hadn't read a book a student wanted to read, I read it, too, just to see what they were into. Then I added it to my list of suggestions!

3 As an example, the game Spelling Bee from *The New York Times* hits right in my zone of proximal development: I know enough words that I can play the game with ease, but I can't consistently figure out the pangram before I hit the paywall. This challenge keeps me interested and coming back to play every day.

4 I want to mention the work of Stuart Brown, a medical doctor who studied play in animals. I saw him at a conference – aptly named The Play Conference – in Los Angeles. He is an advocate for fostering play in school and his work had an influence on how I thought about instruction.

5 At the end of the book, you'll find checklists and prompts to help you plan your year using the tools in this chapter. If you were in my class, we'd create a learning experience that would feel way more engaging, but alas, we're meeting in this 2D world!

Works Cited

Appelt, Kathi. *The Underneath*. Atheneum, 2008.

Deci, Edward L. and Ryan, Richard M. "Facilitating Optimal Motivation and Psychological Well-Being across Life's Domains". *Canadian Psychology*. Vol 49, Issue 1, pp 14–23, 2008.

Gaiman, Neil. *Neverwhere*. Avon Books, 1996.

Gay, Roxane. "To Scratch, Claw, Or Grope Clumsily Or Frantically". *Bad Feminist*. Harper Perennial, 2014, pp 29–43.

Goldstein, Dana. "In the Fight over How to Teach Reading, This Guru Makes a Major Retreat". www.nytimes.com/2022/05/22/us/reading-teaching-curriculum-phonics.html. Accessed 31 May 2022.

"John Dewey's Pedagogy: A Summary". www.teachthought.com/learning/pedagogy-john-dewey-summary/. Accessed 13 May 2022.

Link, Kelly. "Monster". *Pretty Monsters*. Speak, 2008.

Maslow, Abraham H. "A Theory of Human Motivation (Chapter 2)". *Motivation and Personality*. 3rd Edition, Harper & Row, 1954, pp 15–31.

McDaniels, Darryl "DMC". "Angel". *The Moth: 50 True Stories*, edited by Carol Burns. Hachett Books, 2013, pp 140–147.

McLeod, Saul Dr. "The Zone of Proximal Development and Scaffolding". Updated 2019. https://www.simplypsychology.org/Zone-of-Proximal-Development.html. Accessed 20 May 2022.

Morgenstern, Erin. *Night Circus*. Anchor Books, 2011.

"Reading and Writing Project". *Reading and Writing Project*. https://readingandwritingproject.org/. Accessed 16 May 2022.

Satrapi, Marjane. *Persepolis*. Pantheon, June 2004.

Stoker, Bram. *Dracula*. Wordsworth Editions Limited, 1997.

Stone, Nic. *Clean Getaway*. Crown Books for Young Readers, 2020.

"Units of Study: Reading, Writing, Phonics". www.unitsofstudy.com/. Accessed 16 May 2022.

Wiggins, Grant and McTigue, Jay. *Understanding by Design*. 2nd Edition, Pearson, 2015.

Willems, Mo. *The Pigeon Finds a Hot Dog*. Hyperion Books for Children, May 2004.

4

Joyful Assessment

As I start this chapter, it might be useful to clarify the terms I'm using. When I use "assessment", I mean the methods or tools used to identify and measure students' progress toward a learning goal. When I use the term "grade", I mean the act of evaluating the extent to which a student has progressed toward the learning target and then assigning that progress a letter grade.

Learning Targets

If I had known about and fully appreciated learning targets as a young teacher, my teaching practice would have looked drastically different. I was hobbled by ignorance and it's a shame for the kids I taught back then. I apologize to each and every one of them. Instead, learning targets came to me late in my career as a result of studying competency-based practices. I can't pinpoint one book that helped me more than others; rather, each book supplied a new ingredient for my recipe. So here's a list of books that influenced how I thought about the process of assessing student work:

- *On Your Mark: Challenging the Conventions of Grading and Reporting*, by Thomas R. Guskey (2015)
- *A Repair Kit for Grading: 15 Fixes for Broken Grades*, by Ken O'Connor (2011)
- *Grading for Equity* by Joe Feldman (2019)

DOI: 10.4324/9781003374909-4

- *Competency-Based Education: A New Architecture for K-12 Schooling* by Rose Colby (2017)
- *Breaking with Tradition: The Shift to Competency-Based Learning in PLCs at Work* by Brian M. Stack and Jonathan G. Vander Els (2018)
- *Leaders of Their Own Learning* by Ron Berger, Leah Rugen, and Libby Woodfin (2014)

I've listed the books in the order I'd recommend reading them to build and refine understanding. Also, I'm sure there are other great books out there that are only about learning targets…I just haven't read them yet.

Learning targets describe – in brief, kid-friendly language – what students will *know* or be *able to do* as a result of a unit of study. In other words, learning targets, by describing the purpose of lessons or units, focus student effort. They are similar to standards or learning outcomes with the key difference being that learning targets are written to be used by students. When you write a learning target well, even the youngest student should understand why they are working on a particular activity or project.

Here's an example of a learning target for 4th grade science:

I can accurately weigh liquids and solids.

Here's one for 8th grade algebra:

I can apply the order of operations to the evaluation of expressions.

As you can see, the statements are really simple and written from the student perspective. They are used to both organize the scope of work and to evaluate work students turn in for grading. For my 8th grade English class, I had five writing learning targets and three reading learning targets for the entire school year. I used the same three writing learning targets for the first half of the year, then, as students moved into the proficiency or mastery range of the first three skills, I added the remaining skills, one at a time.

Learning targets organize the scope of work by signaling to students what it is they should focus on as they practice. So, in the first half of the year in my English class, students worked to master only three writing skills: big idea, detail, and mechanics. These are significant skills, of course, and it takes quite a bit of practice to master them. But by telling students upfront what I expected them to learn, they could put all their effort into those three skills rather than worrying about the other elements that could go into a paper. In subjects like math, the learning targets will change more frequently, as new skills that build on prior knowledge are introduced more frequently.

Interestingly, I heard from a Marzano educator that teachers should aim for no more than 20 significant learning targets in one year, recognizing that those 20 main skills contain sub-skills which must be identified and outlined. Regardless, the idea here is that when students can focus their attention on just a few skills at a time, they will show more progress. Dance teachers and coaches know this already, as they don't ask their athletes to, say, perfect their tendús at the same time as they perfect jetés. One skill must be mastered before the next can be accomplished. Limiting the scope of work also makes student progress visible *to the students*, which helps students experience the joy that comes from mastering a skill.

Learning targets are extra handy when it is time to evaluate student performance. You simply write a rubric that shows the steps involved in mastery of the learning target. For example, if the following was my learning target:

I can write a story or essay with a purpose--or **big idea**--in mind.

This is my rubric:
You can see that the beginning level descriptor is what a student might say if they were a complete novice with the skill: they might have a story in mind, but they don't know the purpose of the story. Then, as understanding of the big idea develops, students might know the purpose of the story, but they haven't included that purpose in what they wrote (developing level). Each box, reading from right to left, represents the journey a learner takes from knowing nothing about big ideas to mastering big ideas in their writing. I should add here that some people are put off by the word "mastery"…they think it means that students have to become experts in the skill, like Serena Williams is a master tennis player. But I don't expect my 8th grade students to write as skillfully as Roxane Gay or George Saunders! Instead, mastery of "big idea" at an 8th grade level might look like what is described in the

Mastery	Proficient	Developing	Beginning
My big idea is original and piques reader interest. The big idea is clear, present throughout the work, and guides the details.	My big idea is original and helps the reader understand the purpose of the piece. It is clear and present throughout the work.	I know what the big idea is, but I haven't made it clear in the writing, so the reader doesn't know what I'm writing about.	I can't really figure out what the big idea is.

"mastery" box: the big idea is present, it's original, and it guides the details of the work.

I'll explain rubrics more in the next chapter on grading, but it's worth mentioning that in order to properly assess progress, you need a rubric for each learning target.

Formative and Summative Assessment

Formative assessment is *practice* of a skill. Classwork is formative assessment. At its best and most authentic purpose, homework is formative assessment. Any work students put into learning a skill that isn't included in the term grade is formative assessment. While this practice is not graded – as it is unfair to assign a grade while students are still learning a skill – feedback is given so that the student can learn and progress.

Summative assessment is the end-of-the-chapter or unit assessment that *will* be a part of the term grade. In practice, summative assessments tend to be cumulative and cover a collection of skills rather than just a few. But in theory, summative assessment really just means it's the assessment that will "count".

I bring up formative and summative assessment because a thorough understanding has implications for grading. For example, if we agree that formative assessment shouldn't be graded because it is inappropriate and deleterious to grade students as they learn, then *homework shouldn't be a part of a student's grade*. Indeed, understanding that homework is formative assessment means that we should reconsider the entire notion of homework. If it's practice, isn't that practice best done under the supervision and guidance of the teacher, who can give immediate, corrective feedback before inaccurate patterns and misunderstandings are reinforced through repetition? Instead of assigning work to do at home, use class time to practice. To accommodate this, the explanations, instructions, and demonstrations that normally take up class time can be kept very short – less than ten minutes – or delivered via video and watched at home.

Further, if we agree that summative assessment is the assessment that will be counted in the term grade, that means you don't have to jam ten skills into one long test; rather, you can focus on assessing progress a few skills at a time, which has the added benefit of being a more accurate method of measurement. Summative assessments should only be undertaken when it's clear all students have mastered the content or skill. Again, this has practical implications for grading, as you have to determine how long it takes students in your grade level to master a particular skill and align that learning progression to the term length. For example, if you know it takes about six weeks of practice for students to master dividing fractions and your term is eight weeks long, then the summative assessment for dividing fractions should happen at the end of week six. That gives you time to grade the assessments and offer students the opportunity to revise their work before you submit grades.

Here's how formative and summative assessment looked in my class:

◆ Formative assessment happened daily as activities, writing practice, and brief discussions. I used class time for students to practice and share their results, over and over and over again. In this way, students received feedback not only from me, but from their peers (which also serves to strengthen relationships among students). Because I made sure I heard from every student, almost every class, I had a well-developed understanding of what individuals had learned so far, how deep their learning was, and what feedback I could provide to help them progress. Additionally, because I knew what the summative assessment would be, all formative assessment was designed to lead students to success on the summative assessment. As an example, if the summative assessment was to write about adventure, the activities that led up to that assignment involved *how* to write adventures: describing action sequences, foreshadowing, building tension, and crafting satisfying conclusions. I was also clear with the students about the purpose of practice by saying something like, "An adventure needs action! Today, we're going to practice how to write clear but exciting action sequences". The goal was that students could repurpose the pieces that they wrote in class for their summative assessment. I just want to add that students tend not to grumble about practice when they see how it serves their graded work. Feeling as though your work has a purpose is also a source of joy.

◆ My summative assessments were papers or projects. Students knew what the summative assessment was six to ten weeks in advance, and every assignment in the ensuing weeks served as practice for that assessment. The papers weren't very long…as 8th graders, my students could usually manage about three to five (double-spaced) pages of writing before the wheels fell off. I gave word totals instead of page counts as a guideline…1,500 words took ten weeks and meant students focused on 500 words at a time. The timeline was dependent on the complexity of the assignment; 800–1,000 words merited a four to six week timeline. Before the final product was due, I provided feedback in written *and* video form, so students had time to improve specific areas before the work was graded. Finally, summative assessments covered the learning targets I had outlined for the students and that they had been practicing for the preceding weeks. Of course, writing involves all sorts of skills – like tone, voice, pacing, and flow – but I only looked at the skills described in the learning targets. The source of joy in these summative assessments was that they were chosen by the students, they grew from connections students had made between ideas, and they were a demonstration of students' mastery of skills.

I'm going to expand on grading in the next chapter, but it's worth noting that the only assessments I graded were summative assessments, and that the term-end grade only included summative assessment scores. This meant that the summative assessments had to be high quality and authentic...in other words, a multiple-choice or short answer "test" wouldn't cut it. Students needed to produce work that demonstrated their progress in real-world writing like short fiction, narratives, or essays.

Performance-Based Assessment

Performance-based assessment is when you evaluate the actual "performance" of the targeted skill. An excellent example of this is the in-car driving test that all people who want a driver's license in the United States must pass. The reason drivers have to pass an in-car test is that one can know the rules of the road in theory – assessed with a multiple-choice exam – but applying them in a moving vehicle is a different matter. My bias is that secondary assessment should be performance-based whenever possible because application of knowledge is more engaging and long-lasting than memorization. Another analogy I've heard is that you can teach kids baseball skills like batting and catching, but eventually you have to let them play a game. The game is the performance assessment.

In an English class, the "performance" is the paper or the speech or the presentation. In science, it's testing your hypothesis by conducting an experiment you've designed. In history, the performance is participating in a debate or simulation that requires application of skills like developing arguments and offering appropriate evidence. In a world language, the performance could be using the target language to dine at a restaurant (which covers speaking, listening, and reading), while in math a performance-based assessment might be calculating the costs of a trip to the market for groceries or designing a garden.

What I like about performance-based assessments is that they require the application of knowledge and skills. As a result, they are far more meaningful, relevant, and yes, even joyful for students. Performance-based assessment can be used for both formative and summative purposes. For example, dancers have to practice a movement many times as the teacher provides feedback (formative). Then, when it's time for the final performance, in front of an audience, that movement is evaluated as part of a larger routine (summative).

One of the more joyful performance-based assessments I offered was a summative assessment I gave as the "final exam". In the particular year I'm thinking of, my students still read all the same books. The learning target for their literature study was to derive meaning from the books and apply those lessons to their own lives. The essential question for that year was the one I mentioned in Chapter 3:

> In the face of monsters, madness, and mayhem, what makes life worth living?

Meanwhile, the writing learning targets centered on big ideas, specific details, mechanics, descriptive language, and voice.

For this particular performance-based assessment, I told students they were invited to a dinner party in the classroom. However, they had to come to class and interact with one another as a character from one of the books we'd read that year. For example, one student was Jack from *Lord of the Flies*, while another student was Miles from Kelly Link's story "The Wrong Grave". Further requirements were:

1 As the character, they had to write a series of questions for the other characters in the room…the kind of questions you'd ask if you were trying to get to know another person.
2 As the character, they had to write an answer to the essential question.
3 As themselves, they had to write about what they learned that year in English that they didn't know before.

At the in-class dinner party, students shared their answers to the essential question as well as what they learned.

Each students' work product was brilliant in its own way. The student who was assigned Miles wrote all three of his assignments as haikus, a form of poetry the character Miles employs to hilarious effect in "The Wrong Grave". It was clear this student had mastered the learning target of voice. Another student, whose character was an artist, created a piece of art that answered the essential question (supplemented by a written response) and showed she understood big ideas. The beautiful work done by the students moved me.

Through their performances, students demonstrated all the skills they had mastered over the course of the year while also creating meaning, relevance, humor, and joy.

Summary

- ◆ Developing 10–20 student-friendly learning targets for the year is an effective way to ensure student progress.
- ◆ Formative assessment – practice – should be the focus of instructional time.
- ◆ Summative assessment – work included in the term grade – should be guided by the learning targets and should be focused on a few skills at a time.
- ◆ Performance-based assessments require application of knowledge and skills through completion of specific tasks. They are driven by learning targets and can be both formative and summative in nature.
- ◆ Assessment of all types is more joyful when students have some degree of choice in the assessment, as this imbues the assessment with meaning.
- ◆ When the students see their skills improve as a result of the assessment, they experience the joy of mastery, which develops confidence.
- ◆ Assessment can be an experience of community, connection, play, humor, and optimism. In fact, this is assessment at its best.

Learning Targets for My 8th Grade English Class

Writing

For the First Half of the Year
1. I can write a story or essay with a purpose – or big idea – in mind.
I can explain my big idea using specific details or examples.
I can write using accurate spelling, proper punctuation and capitalization, and clear sentence structure.
Once the First Three Have Been Mastered I Add…
I can write using descriptive language that communicates an image, emotion, or memory.
I can write using a distinct voice I've developed.

Reading

I am an engaged and motivated reader.
2. I can identify the big ideas of a written work.
I can make connections between the big idea of a written work and my own life.

Works Cited

Berger, Ron, Ruger, Leah and Woodfin, Libby. *Leaders of Their Own Learning: Transforming Schools through Student-Engaged Assessment*. 1st Edition, Jossey-Bass, 2014.

Colby, Rose. *Competency-Based Education: A New Architecture for K-12 Schooling*. Harvard Education Press, 2017.

Feldman, Joe. *Grading for Equity*. 1st Edition, Corwin, 2018.

Golding, William. *Lord of the Flies*. Penguin Reissue Edition, 1959.

Guskey, Thomas. *On Your Mark: Challenging the Conventions of Grading and Reporting*. Solution Tree Press, 2015.

Link, Kelly. "The Wrong Grave". *Pretty Monsters*. Speak, 2008.

Marzano, Robert, Norford, Jennifer and Ruyle, Mike. *The New Art and Science of Classroom Assessment*. Solution Tree Press 2019.

O'Connor, Ken. *A Repair Kit for Grading: 15 Fixes for Broken Grades*. Allyn & Bacon, 2010.

Stack, Brian M. and Vander Els, Jonathan G. *Breaking with Tradition: The Shift to Competency-Based Learning in PLCs at Work*. Solution Tree Press, 2017.

5

Joyful Grading

Grading is the heart of what we do in school. Indeed, in traditional schools where students earn grades, the grades tend to become the focus. It's frustrating, because, of course, as teachers we want our students to love learning. At the same time, students respond to the system we adults have set up for them, which is to strive for high grades because high grades, in our society, apparently equal success in all kinds of endeavors, from college to jobs to life itself.

My thinking about grading has significantly evolved over the years, mostly due to my study of competency-based learning. I point out the same books I mentioned in Chapter 4 as guideposts for reconsidering traditional notions about grades:

- ◆ *On Your Mark: Challenging the Conventions of Grading and Reporting*, by Thomas R. Guskey (2015)
- ◆ *A Repair Kit for Grading: 15 Fixes for Broken Grades*, by Ken O'Connor (2011)
- ◆ *Grading for Equity* by Joe Feldman (2019)
- ◆ *Competency-Based Education: A New Architecture for K-12 Schooling* by Rose Colby (2017)
- ◆ *Breaking with Tradition: The Shift to Competency-Based Learning in PLCs at Work* by Brian M. Stack and Jonathan G. Vander Els (2018)
- ◆ *Leaders of Their Own Learning* by Ron Berger, Leah Rugen, and Libby Woodfin (2014).

DOI: 10.4324/9781003374909-5

In this chapter, I present the processes I developed for my students based on my takeaways from the above books. My goal, as I made each change, was to help students understand what grades are comprised of and thereby create meaning. When grades are meaningful to the students, the process of earning those grades – striving and learning – is joyful, as joy comes from a sense of mastery, connection, agency, and purpose.

Feedback that Fosters Growth

When I was a new teacher, I thought feedback happened when I graded papers, as in, students would write their work and turn it in to me, then I'd write feedback on the papers and grade them at the same time. If students wanted to improve their work, their only choice was to apply the comments to the next paper…but, of course, the next paper would ask for a little something different in terms of content and skills. This practice was what I knew from my own years as a student and it didn't occur to me to wonder about it until I had been teaching for some time. But now, looking back, I cringe in embarrassment at my flawed, rather harmful mode of evaluation. It's completely unfair to grade an attempt. If anything, I *decelerated* my students' improvement because I didn't give them a chance to get it right before I slapped a grade on the work. And, as I mentioned in Chapter 1, because I had no rubric or learning targets, my grades were based on a dim understanding in my own head; I pretty much made them up!

Eventually, I created a system in which students practiced a particular skill, wrote a draft of a paper using that skill, and then I gave multiple rounds of feedback on the drafts. Students submitted a thoroughly edited paper for grading. Additionally, I allowed students to rewrite their work for a higher grade at any point in the year. In approximately 22 years of allowing rewrites, one student asked me to revise a paper from a previous trimester, which meant I had to submit a grade change request to the school office. I allowed it and, luckily, my principal didn't have a problem with it, either. If that student really wanted to go back to an assignment from ten weeks ago, who am I to tell them no? I admire the drive! But, the truth is, once you start the practice of providing tons of feedback as students work, they don't need to revise as much once the work has been graded. By the time I graded a paper, it had already been rewritten two or three times.

For feedback to be effective, it must be *frequent*, *timely*, and *targeted*. *Frequent* means that you create enough checkpoints as students do their work that even if they veer a bit off course, you can correct them before they totally spin out. As an example, in my class, I had students write their papers in chunks, and I'd check one part before I asked them to move on to other parts. I spoke daily with every student, and I was conscientious about pointing out what they did well rather than focusing on what was missing. *Timely* means that students need feedback in time for that feedback to make a difference in their performance. This translated into me providing feedback multiple times *before* a final draft was due for grading. In other words, each draft of a paper was a formative assessment, while the final version of the paper – the one that I graded – was the summative assessment. Lastly, *targeted* feedback means that you only comment on the learning targets. It's tempting to provide feedback on all the components of a work product, but this can be confusing for students. If you say format doesn't matter but then circle all the non-indented sentences at the start of paragraphs – as though you'd like them corrected – is format being assessed or not? Keep your comments focused on the learning targets outlined in the assignment guidelines.

As you give feedback, it's also worth considering how students best receive your comments and then act on what you told them. The Holy Grail of feedback is an in-person meeting between student and teacher, in which teachers can thoroughly explain themselves and ask questions of the students. However, in-person meetings are time-consuming and aren't always practical when you're trying to get work back to students quickly. A breakthrough for me in delivering the best possible feedback to students was the browser extension Loom. Loom gives you the capability to create a video of yourself speaking to your student about their paper *while that paper is on your computer screen*! So as I speak to the student via audio recording, I can highlight various areas of the paper or I can scroll to the comment I already wrote and explain it more thoroughly. It's really cool, and the end result is a little video, stored in the cloud, that you can embed in the student's paper. Students click the link to get video narration of your comments. My students told me that they found this mode very helpful because they could read what I wrote and then listen to me explain it. Also, they could replay the video if they missed any part or wanted to double check their understanding. On my end, I felt like I could get through each paper faster because I wasn't struggling as much with the written comments. Lastly, after I introduced Loom, students made more effective revisions, which I attribute to their increased comprehension of the feedback. My epiphany about Loom was that, in 2021, my students had grown up spending their time *watching videos to learn* about subjects of interest rather than *reading to learn* about subjects of interest. Loom videos tap into that audio-visual learning mode, which is a win for teachers.

Effective feedback contributes to joyful learning because when students know exactly how to improve, they're able to make their work product better. In other words, they're able to move closer to mastery of a particular skill or demonstration of knowledge. It's quite gratifying for students to feel that they've practiced and shown improvement; conversely, practicing without proper feedback to improve is the worst kind of drudgery, akin to pushing a boulder up a hill just to have it roll back down again. Feedback is the fertilizer that helps growth occur, which in turn cultivates meaning and joy.

Writing Rubrics That Work

When I first tried my hand at creating rubrics for my 8th grade English students' papers, I had fanciful--and mistaken--ideas about what should be in a rubric. One of the categories was "apprehension of the luminous"…as in James Joyce's beautiful line from *Portrait of the Artist as a Young Man*. Sadly, I'm not kidding. That phrase has stayed with me since I first encountered it 32 years ago, and I was excited to introduce this concept to my 8th graders. I thought it was whimsical and fun, but it also somehow captured what I wanted to see in their writing: creativity and an exploration of what they found beautiful. I came up with four descriptors and laid out the criteria. As it turned out, including "apprehension of the luminous" on the rubric not only baffled my students and teaching partner, but it also failed to produce stronger, more idiosyncratic writing.

Offering feedback that fosters growth is one of the most important aspects of our jobs as teachers. Obviously, asking 13–14 year olds to "apprehend the luminous" in their writing was not a great strategy for growth! But eventually, after many iterations and lots of student input, I figured out how to create rubrics that helped my students understand what was expected of them and evaluate their progress in a meaningful, authentic way. As a result, students felt more invested and were happy to be in class.

The key concept in rubric writing is clarifying its purpose. As a younger teacher, I misunderstood the job of a rubric: I thought it was a tool to assist me in grading. However, after deep reading and professional development about competency-based learning, I reframed the rubric's purpose as *a tool to provide feedback to the* **student** *about their progress toward mastery of a learning target*. This shift changed everything! By centering student growth, I was able to provide specific feedback that my students could understand and easily implement. It was a miracle.

My next revelation was that generating feedback that fosters growth is a project in backwards design. Here are the steps:

1   Develop clear learning targets for students written in language they can understand. I had made the mistake of using needlessly complicated language to describe learning objectives that were, frankly, written for me as the teacher rather than for the students, i.e., "Students will generate a provable, arguable thesis". When I switched to the student perspective, i.e., "I can write an essay or story with a purpose--big idea--in mind", what was expected was much clearer to the student.

   As mentioned, my other big mistake was over-complicating the rubric with learning targets that couldn't be quantified and that ultimately didn't matter. "Apprehending the luminous" still sounds fantastic to me, but now I leave it off the rubric and hope it is a joyful byproduct of writing.

2   Consider which sub-skills or knowledge support the learning target. For example, including "textual evidence" in an essay means that you also have to *identify* what counts as textual evidence for a particular thesis. This sub-skill should be delineated on the rubric.

3   When writing a four-point rubric, use the descriptor boxes to lay out, in order, the steps of skill acquisition. I think of a "4" as mastery of the skill and "1" as a person who's not encountered the skill before…a novice. When one is a novice, what does practice of the skill look like? What components are present and what is absent? What does the skill look like at a "2" level? Some people find it helpful to begin by describing the "4" or mastery level, and then take away components as they move down a level in each descriptor box. The goal here is that when students look at the rubric, they should see how learning progresses as they master a skill.

   When I wrote rubrics before I knew about learning targets, I didn't understand exactly what I was doing; I had a hard time writing the descriptor boxes, as not every "A" or "B" paper looked the same. The words that literally changed my understanding of rubrics are that they should describe the *progression of learning in the targeted skill*. For some reason, these words just clicked in my brain and I could see what I had been doing wrong in every other rubric I'd written. This was an exciting development for me and an even better development for the students, as they could finally understand the rubric that I used to determine their grade.

4 Check your work. Once you've written the rubric, give it to students and seek their feedback. Do they understand the words? Can they apply it to other kids' work? Then, can they apply it to their own? Make adjustments based on what the students have to say about the rubric's utility.

5 Check your work again. Use the student work that has been submitted to you to quality-check the rubric's descriptors: have you captured each component of mastery? Did you adequately qualify the difference between a "4" and "3"? A "1" and "2"? Make adjustments.

Once you've developed a clear rubric, consider how to use it effectively.

My first tip for effective rubric use is that you must use the language of the rubric when you offer feedback. I often made the mistake of using words like "details" and "support" and "examples" interchangeably in my comments, thinking my students followed along. Some of them did, but a

Criteria	Mastery	Proficient	Developing	Beginning
I can write using descriptive language that communicates an image, emotion, or memory.	The words I chose skillfully communicate an emotion, image, or memory that helps the reader understand and connect to the writing. I chose these words with care and used them deliberately. My writing is vividly descriptive and I show what's happening rather than tell.	The words I chose communicate an emotion, image, or memory that helps the reader understand. The words are deliberate. My writing is descriptive and I tend to show what is happening rather than tell.	The words I chose at times communicate an emotion, image, or memory that helps the reader understand. Occasionally, I use descriptive language. I tend to tell what is happening rather than show.	The words I chose do not call on emotion, imagery, or memory to help convey meaning. I do not use descriptive language.

few of them didn't, which served to frustrate those kids. When I switched to using consistent language in the rubric *and* the feedback, I saw an immediate improvement in the students' ability to revise as expected.

The second tip is that once students have revised, ask them to explain their process to you. Hearing the rationale about why students made the changes they did (or didn't) is eye-opening, as it allows you to see the relationship between student understanding and application. Through these meetings, I realized how frequently my comment of "give an example here" or "this is awkwardly worded" didn't make sense to the student. Having the opportunity to clarify and revise any misunderstandings is useful to you and to the student's learning. If time for meetings is short, students could make a Loom video explaining their rationale to you.

Rubrics used in my class are at the end of this chapter.

Revision

In the previous section, I briefly mentioned the notion of revision and that I asked my students to not only revise their work multiple times before submitting it for grading, but that I allowed revisions after grading, as well.

All teachers should figure out how to work revision into summative as well as formative assessments. This is best practice. I think of it like this: if my goal is to help students progress in their skills and develop resilience as they problem solve, then the way to do that is through providing endless opportunities to learn from mistakes *without those mistakes having a negative impact on grades*. Students care so much about their grades because that's the system schools have created; unfortunately, for most students grades are a source of self-worth and identity. It's unethical, I think, to ask students to take risks or really push themselves when they are worried about how failure will affect their course grade, but we can remove the negative impact of failure by encouraging revision! Yes, it is more work, and the results are *totally* worth the effort.

You can build revision into your grading process by considering the following:

◆ Projects are a great way to assess, because they tend to be more engaging for students and they also bundle key skills. Break your projects into tiny little steps that you check, so students have a chance to revise before they get to the end of their work. In my experience, students are much more willing to revise work that was just completed than work that was completed weeks ago.

◆ If projects don't work for your class and you give tests instead, consider giving the test in stages that build. In this way, you can provide feedback on each of the stages and students can use that information to improve their work on the next stage. For example, if you ask students to memorize where all the countries in Africa are located, have them just identify a few countries at a time. Check whether they're right or wrong, then have them proceed. This methodology also capitalizes on the connective, relational aspects of memory. Similarly, if you group problems on your math assessments by concept, students can complete a section of the assessment, get feedback, and learn from their mistakes *before* they move on to the next section that requires the accurate use of those skills.

◆ Plan revision time into the course schedule. For example, if you have the summative assessment/project due two to three weeks before the term ends, that gives you about a week to grade and return the work to students, a week for the students to revise and resubmit before the grading period ends, and a few days for you to review the edited work.

◆ When students revise their work, just have them focus on the problems they got wrong or on the pieces of the project that need improvement. Similarly, when you re-grade, just look at the edited work. I know math teachers who dread having to rewrite a carefully crafted test. There's no need to write another test; just have the student re-do the incorrect problems.

◆ Give full credit for work that was re-done correctly. 25 years ago, I was advised to give partial credit to revised work in the interest of "fairness" to the other students, who "got it right the first time". The thing is, I'm not down with only rewarding "getting it right the first time". The time it takes to learn a skill is inconsequential. What matters is the progress students can make by learning from their mistakes. Full credit, all the way.

◆ Effective revisions are linked to effective feedback. When your feedback is clear and targeted, students know what to do. When your feedback is vague or too general, students struggle to apply it. If the edited work is not an improvement, consider how to tweak your feedback and communicate more clearly with each student.

Learning where one's mistakes lie and being able to immediately implement the correction also helps develop grit, an educational buzzword from around 2016, but one that is still relevant. While grit itself perhaps isn't joyful, the capacity to persist and succeed at a task can create a sense of mastery, which is a source of joy. As a result, revision that leads to measurable improvement is immensely satisfying for students.

Get Rid of the Average, Zeros, and Grades that Don't Matter

Other writers, with statistics and research to back up their reasoning, have written eloquently about why the traditional grading system of percentages, letter grades, and grades as coercion is not only flawed, but inequitable and harmful. I've mentioned these authors twice already, but here they are again and I really hope you pick up these books:

◆ *On Your Mark: Challenging the Conventions of Grading and Reporting*, by Thomas R. Guskey (2015)
◆ *A Repair Kit for Grading: 15 Fixes for Broken Grades*, by Ken O'Connor (2011)
◆ *Grading for Equity* by Joe Feldman (2019)

These works deeply resonated with me, as they called out all the problems I'd seen in grading as well as presenting a few scenarios I hadn't encountered before. As a result of reading these books, I changed my grading practices in the following ways:

1 I completely threw out the category grading system I had used for years. Instead, only the summative assessments – papers or projects – were recorded in the gradebook as "counting" toward the term grade. Additionally, I adopted a policy of "highest grade = term grade" (O'Connor 125). This meant that if students wrote three papers in a term, earning grades of B-, A-, and A, the term end grade was the highest of those three grades, or A.

   I did this because averages obscure what's really going on with students' learning. For example, in the category of "writing", if a student earns a B-, an A-, and an A, the average is 89.6%, or an A-. What this grade leaves out is the important fact that the student improved and earned an A as the term progressed. In my "highest grade = term grade" paradigm, what's counted is the student's best performance of the targeted skill. What's important is that the student mastered the skill. The grade should reflect that mastery.

2 A natural consequence of only including summative assessments in the term grade was that quizzes no longer "counted". Students still took vocabulary quizzes, but it was as a chosen check on their understanding rather than a way to impact the term grade.

3 I no longer gave writing homework because it wasn't a part of the term grade. Consequently, all writing was done in class. This was a success on many fronts, but the most significant impact is that I was able to give students immediate feedback and help them when they were "stuck".

I had stopped giving zeros for missing work a long time prior (O'Connor 95). It just didn't feel fair to decimate a student's grade because they hadn't turned in an assignment. It was my fault for not following up in time or not making the assignment compelling enough in the first place! However, many of my colleagues used zeros as an incentive to turn in missing work. I implore you not to do this; it has a negative impact on your relationship with students and, according to Guskey's research, it doesn't actually work in the long term ("Are Zeros Your Ultimate Weapon" 33).

It was such a relief to get rid of grades that didn't matter, like journals and quizzes. The grades on report cards finally represented students' progress in targeted writing skills. I recognize that classes like math use quizzes as a check-in to see whether students understand certain concepts or have mastered the skills. However, I'd argue these quizzes should be formative rather than summative…in other words, the quizzes shouldn't be counted in the term grade. Quizzes are practice (O'Connor 106–115)!

While I made these grading changes because they were equitable practices that made sense, there was also a discernible impact on student satisfaction with my class. Specifically, students understood the grading system, they knew exactly where their grades came from, and they felt the grades to be fair, which they reported made them feel happy because I was on their "side". Further, when students can see the direct connection between the work they do in class and the mark on their report cards, they feel grades are authentic and relevant, which is a source of happiness.

Get the Kids Involved

The most impactful change I made in my grading practice was getting my students directly involved in the grading effort. My gestures toward student-centered grading in the past were rather weak tea: i.e., peer evaluation, writing a sentence about how they think they did at the end of the assignment, or writing a narrative for themselves at the end of each grading term. I don't mean to be dismissive…each of these practices emboldened me to strive for more meaningful engagement from the students. But the students experienced these efforts as just another hoop they had to jump through for inexplicable reasons. I had read about the joyful empowerment to be had from student-centered grading, and I craved that meaning and delight for my students. All that was needed, I felt, was a clearly articulated, easy to execute process.

To my surprise, though, the most powerful barrier to the change I sought in this realm was the students themselves. When I explained to my students that I wanted them to evaluate and grade their own work, they groaned. They rolled their eyes. They said, "That's *your* job". So I have to admit, sheepishly, that I used middle school tactics against my poor students: I brought up self-assessment so many times during the course of the year that I finally wore them down and they agreed to grade just ONE assignment themselves. And that one assignment was all it took to hook them. They loved it. The following school year, I was able to start with student-centered assessment and refine the process.

Here are the steps I took:

1   I revised my learning targets to ensure that they were written in kid language and focused on only one skill.
2   In the first month of school, I focused on teaching the language of the learning targets, so students truly understood what a "big idea" or "supporting detail" looked like in their written work. It was all play-based and silly, but it helped students get familiar with the language we used for assessments.
3   I had students practice evaluating each other's work before they evaluated themselves. As a result, students learned to look for evidence of the learning targets.
4   For the first half of the year, I used the same rubric for all written assessments. This really helped, as the guideposts weren't constantly changing and the learning target language was being imprinted onto the students' understanding of writing.
5   Before students evaluated their own work, I provided written and recorded audio feedback about the learning targets and asked students to revise. In this way, they *already* knew which areas of the work needed improvement and what was strong, so if they edited successfully, they'd have a fair understanding of where the work stood in terms of the rubric.
6   Part of the self-evaluation process was to provide evidence. So, for example, since one of the learning targets was about writing with a purpose, students highlighted where the "big idea" showed up in their stories. This visual really helped students see how well they'd integrated their big ideas into their writing, which meant I didn't have to explain quite as much.
7   I met with each student to review their work and their evaluation.[1] They'd explain their revisions to me, then they'd explain where

they thought their work fell in each category of the rubric, using evidence from their stories. Finally, they'd tell me what grade they thought the work merited, based on what they'd just shared. For example, when all the descriptors met the "mastery" standard, the grade was an "A".

8   In the conferences, I'd support students' self-evaluation as much as possible. At our first meeting, students were typically tentative. They'd rate their work lower on the scale either because they truly weren't sure how well they performed or they underrated themselves for safety. I fully understood their vulnerable position, but I persisted because I felt it was critical for students to be involved in the grading process. Over the course of the school year, students grew accustomed to self-evaluation and therefore were more confident about their ratings. One girl – a gifted writer – never thought what she wrote was good enough, while I thought her work was brilliant. She persisted in pointing out perceived flaws as I doggedly pointed out the ways in which her writing met the criteria for mastery. By the end of the year, I had convinced this student that while she may not be satisfied with all she wrote, her work met or exceeded the learning targets. That felt like a success to me.

    Occasionally, a student's work didn't align with their evaluation of it. In those cases, I'd gently point out how the work could be stronger, then invite the student to rewrite. While all of my students rewrote their work when I asked them to, I have had students who just didn't submit any work at all. That's a completely different problem. In those cases, I'd work with the students and families until I eventually got some work that could be evaluated in time for a grade to be entered. However, I do know of situations in other classes where students had a mark of "incomplete" for their term grade because they didn't submit enough work in the grading period. The expectation is that the work will be made up at some point.

9   The grade that the student and I agreed upon was put into the gradebook.

Once we got this system down, students truly thrived: they *wanted* to push themselves on each assignment with absolutely no coercion or coaxing from me. They were happier, less anxious and stressed, and, ultimately, felt safe and confident in the classroom. Consequently, the students worked hard and made astonishing progress each trimester. No one fell behind or failed, and each student left the class knowing not only that they'd grown, but they also knew *how* they'd grown.

My interpretation of the feedback I received from students – which I collected at multiple points throughout the year – is that students valued the collaborative nature of our work and the support and encouragement they felt from me. They didn't necessarily remember specific instructional practices, but they did remember the quality of our relationship. That's critical, as having a solid relationship with students is the only way you can teach them anything.

And at this point – which was just a few years ago – I felt I had finally achieved a meaningful outcome: my students were invested in their own progress, they knew what they were good at and what could be improved, and they were calm and focused about their work. What's more, they enjoyed the process! Mastery, agency, purpose, connection, positive emotions…these are the ingredients that create joy, and with student self-assessment I had introduced all of those components into class. The result was joyful students and joyful learning.

I must point out that I had the support of administration and my teaching colleagues as I ventured into new grading territory for what had always been a traditional school. Of course, I presented my grading plans to my principal, department chair, and teaching partner beforehand, with the three highlighted, dog-eared books by Guskey, Feldman, and O'Connor by my side. Additionally, my school had asked me to research methods of assessment, so I didn't face significant pushback as I implemented these new practices. Finally, parents were jazzed that their students were doing so well. I was willing to experiment, and I was lucky.

Summary

- Effective feedback is frequent, timely, and targeted.
- Consider the delivery system for feedback and suit it to your audience (i.e., consider both in-person meetings and technology like Loom to create videos for students).
- Rubrics need to include clear learning targets that make sense to students.
- Revision is crucial for learning so it should be built into the process and fully credited.
- Get rid of zeros, averages, and superfluous grades.
- When students see the connection between the work of the class and the mark on the report card, they feel their work is meaningful and relevant, which is joyful.

- ◆ Teach students to evaluate and grade their own work and use those grades.
- ◆ Joy also comes from feeling connected to the grading process and having agency in what the grade outcome will be.

Sample Rubrics from My 8th Grade English Class

Writing Rubric
First Half of Year

	Mastery	Proficient	Developing	Beginning
I can write a story or essay with a big idea – or purpose – in mind.	My big idea is original and piques reader interest. The big idea is clear, present throughout the work, and guides the details.	My big idea is original and helps the reader understand the purpose of the piece. It is clear and present throughout the work.	I know what the big idea is, but I haven't made it clear in the writing, so the reader doesn't know what I'm writing about.	I can't really figure out what the big idea is.
I can explain my big idea using specific details or examples.	The details or examples support and provide evidence for the big idea. The details/examples are layered and make the writing unique to me. Finally, the details/examples help the reader picture what I've described.	Details and examples support and provide evidence for the big idea. Most of the details/examples are specific. Some of the details help the reader picture what I'm writing about.	Details and examples don't all support the big idea. The details are minimal or the examples are not fully explained.	Details and examples do not support the big idea or do not make sense. The descriptions aren't as clear as they could be.

	Mastery	Proficient	Developing	Beginning
I can write using accurate spelling, proper punctuation and capitalization, and clear sentence structure.	There are zero to two spelling, capitalization, punctuation, or grammar in the paper, making it easy to read.	There are three to five errors of grammar, spelling, capitalization, or punctuation in the entire paper. For the most part, the paper is easy to read.	There are enough errors in each paragraph that the paper is hard to understand.	There are so many errors in each paragraph that sentences lose their meaning.

These Skills Are Added One at a Time in Second Half of the Year

Criteria	Mastery	Proficiency	Developing	Beginning
I can write using descriptive language that communicates an image, emotion, or memory.	The words I chose skillfully communicate an emotion, image, or memory that helps the reader understand and connect to the writing. I chose these words with care and used them deliberately. My writing is vividly descriptive and I show what's happening rather than tell.	The words I chose communicate an emotion, image, or memory that helps the reader understand. The words are deliberate. My writing is descriptive and I tend to show what is happening rather than tell.	The words I chose at times communicate an emotion, image, or memory that helps the reader understand. Occasionally, I use descriptive language. I tend to tell what is happening rather than show.	The words I chose do not call on emotion, imagery, or memory to help convey meaning. I do not use descriptive language.

(continued)

Criteria	Mastery	Proficiency	Developing	Beginning
I can create tone through my choice of words, phrases, and sentences.	I craft phrases and sentences purposefully to achieve a particular effect that controls the feeling of the written work (the tone). I can create feelings like irony, suspense, or joy. When other people read my work, the feelings they describe mostly match my intention.	I craft phrases and sentences to control the feeling of the written work. I can create feelings like excitement or fear. Some of the time, other people who read my work can describe the feelings I intended to create.	A few sentences match the feeling I'm striving for. I am not yet able to do this throughout my entire story.	I do not use phrases and sentences to create a particular tone, or feeling, in my written work.

Reading Rubrics
(Please note these are self-evaluations and not included in term grades)

Criteria	Mastery	Proficient	Developing	Beginning
I am an engaged and motivated reader.	When I choose to, I can direct my entire focus into reading and even find that I lose sense of time passing or what's happening around me. I both understand	When I choose to, I can direct my entire focus into reading. I both understand and enjoy the story as it unfolds and may want to share it with another person.	I can direct most of my focus into reading, though I may find myself easily distracted. This distraction means I miss major plot points or themes.	I can direct my focus into reading for brief periods but feel restless while doing so. As a result, I miss much of the story, like major plot points, characters, and themes.

Criteria	Mastery	Proficient	Developing	Beginning
	and enjoy the story as it unfolds and find that I want to share what I read with someone else.			
I can identify the big ideas of a written work.	I can consistently identify a number of big ideas in the reading and support my contentions with evidence from the work in the form of plot, characters, setting, examples, or other details.	I can identify a few big ideas in the reading and support my contentions with evidence from the work in the form of plot, characters, setting, examples, or other details.	At times, I can identify a big idea in the reading. However, I can't always pinpoint support for the big idea.	I am uncertain about the big ideas in what I read.
I can make connections between the big idea of a written work and my own life.	I consistently think about how the big ideas in the reading are present in my life. I can provide details or examples that fully illustrate my point. The connections I make are unique to me.	I think about how the big ideas in the reading are present in my life. I can provide details or examples that fully illustrate my point.	Sometimes I think about how the big ideas in the reading are present in my life. I can usually provide a few examples that illustrate my point.	I can connect a big idea that someone else mentions to my own life, but I often am unclear about where to find examples that illustrate my point.

Note

1 I made meeting with my students a priority, which means that I scheduled the time to do so. As I met with individual students, I had the rest of the class working on their *next* project. I definitely had to plan carefully, but we didn't lose instructional time as a result of the individual meetings. It was important to me that students were a part of the grading process; otherwise, what's the point?

Works Cited

Berger, Ron, Ruger, Leah and Woodfin, Libby. *Leaders of Their Own Learning: Transforming Schools through Student-Engaged Assessment*. 1st Edition, Jossey-Bass, 2014.

Colby, Rose. *Competency-Based Education: A New Architecture for K-12 Schooling*. Harvard Education Press, 2017.

Feldman, Joe. *Grading for Equity*. 1st Edition, Corwin, 2018.

Guskey, Thomas. "Are Zeros Your Ultimate Weapon - Gbcsacc.weebly.com". Weebly.com, Principal Leadership. gbcsacc.weebly.com/uploads/1/4/6/5/14650352/are_zeros_your_ultimate_weapon.pdf. Accessed 16 May 2022.

Guskey, Thomas. *On Your Mark: Challenging the Conventions of Grading and Reporting*. Solution Tree Press, 2015.

Joyce, James. *Portrait of the Artist as a Young Man*. Wordsworth Editions Limited, Revised Edition, 1997.

Marzano, Robert, Norford, Jennifer and Ruyle, Mike. *The New Art and Science of Classroom Assessment*. Solution Tree Press 2019.

O'Connor, Ken. *A Repair Kit for Grading: 15 Fixes for Broken Grades*. Allyn & Bacon, 2010.

Stack, Brian M. and Vander Els, Jonathan G. *Breaking with Tradition: The Shift to Competency-Based Learning in PLCs at Work*. Solution Tree Press, 2017.

6

Joyful Assignments

Joyful learning experiences are built day by day, lesson by lesson. The seemingly small choices you make about lessons, activities, and assignments create the foundation for the students' experience of meaning, relevance, and connection. Consequently, you have to rethink the approach you take to every moment of class.

In Chapter 3, I wrote about the shifts I made in the curriculum that contribute to joy, while in Chapters 4 and 5 I discussed corresponding changes I made to assessment and grading. These changes, of course, meant that I had to retool what happened as students entered the classroom each day. So, as I planned instruction, I asked myself these questions:

- How can I infuse this activity with a spirit of play?
- How can I provide choice in this assignment?
- How can I provide the opportunity for students to work at an appropriate level of challenge?

A Spirit of Play

I found that framing activities were an effective way to squeeze play into class. In my teaching youth, I didn't give much thought at all to framing the lesson objective. It wasn't the important part to me...I wanted to get to the lesson

DOI: 10.4324/9781003374909-6

itself! Now, I really like to give students context for whatever they're going to learn because building background knowledge creates meaning that helps the learning persist over time. Rather than opening class with me talking or pointing at a slide, I create a micro experience that provides context. Here are a few examples of framing activities I've used:

◆ The objective for the day was to understand the theme of "chaos" or "the random nature of the universe". The book the students were reading was *The Hitchhiker's Guide to the Galaxy*, in which a resident of Earth discovers that mice rule the universe. To set this context, I put a few mice into clear plastic hamster balls and set them loose in class. After this, my students were primed to discover the theme of "chaos" or "randomness" in the book![1]

◆ Another day, the objective was to construct an understanding of "perseverance". I set up an obstacle course for the students and asked everyone to attempt it. The course included achievable obstacles that were adaptable to various physical circumstances, like balancing on one foot, passing a Nerf ball to a partner, or transferring small items like plastic spiders from one container to another. All students attempted the course, and they were subsequently able to make a connection between the obstacle course and the big idea of "perseverance".

◆ When the lesson objective was figuring out where "specific details" come from, I started class by asking students to go outside and take a picture of something that captured their attention, like a lovely flower, a reflective shimmer in a puddle, or two kindergartners holding hands. When they came back to class, students shared their photos and talked about what made the images special. Then, I'd ask them to write about the images using the specific details they had just mentioned. Through this framing, students could construct their understanding about where details come from.

◆ About seven years ago, I had a cohort of students who loved drama: many of them acted in the school plays and some even took acting classes outside of school. They were reading *Lord of the Flies* – that stodgy old book – and I really wanted to set the context for an understanding of the role of sacrificial rituals. I dressed in a ridiculous costume comprising my graduation gown, a triangle hat I made inspired by the sorting hat in *Harry Potter*, and about 20 long necklaces that clanged together as I moved. The tech department gave me a nonfunctional iPad to use as a prop. When the students got to class, I told them I was going to sacrifice the iPad to the god of technology, which they clearly honored with their time and attention. I asked students to approach the iPad and make a gesture of obeisance. I muttered nonsense words. Then I pretended to break the iPad. I actually just swapped my working iPad with the one the tech department gave me. This dramatic, completely silly learning experience helped students understand the rituals of sacrifice and then generate connections between the rituals in the book and the ones in their own lives. Recently, a student from that class, Lyle, saw me at a function and brought up my iPad sacrifice. Not only was it cool to see me commit to my character like that, Lyle said, but he also realized learning can be fun. He told me he didn't like reading that much, but watching me flop about in my graduation gown helped him see there might be something valuable in books.

Another objective of the framing activities was to generate positivity and wonder. Consequently, I paid special attention to what made my students laugh, what they chatted about when I wasn't supposed to be listening, and what they looked forward to. With this information, I could use the framing activities to kindle positive emotions like humor, curiosity, and enthusiasm. Entering the classroom in a wizard costume sparks curiosity. Taking pictures of what you find beautiful engenders enthusiasm and awe. When students experienced these positive emotions in the first few minutes of class, it helped to recalibrate their social-emotional landscape so they were more prepared to learn. I mentioned in Chapter 2 that researchers found positive emotions boost self-regulation after ego depletion (Baumeister et al.; Tice et al.). I've certainly found that taking a playful, fun-loving approach to framing activities has a beneficial impact on students' subsequent social-emotional and academic functioning.

To incorporate play into other subjects, I've seen:

◆ Spanish teachers set up "restaurants" in their classrooms so students could practice ordering food in a Spanish-speaking environment.
◆ History teachers create large-scale simulations of political conventions so students can understand "planks" and "platforms".
◆ Algebra teachers custom-make games that require students to apply algebraic equations to real-world scenarios.

Providing Choice in Assignments

When considering choice in assignments it's important to ensure that the various options all lead students to success in the same learning objective. In practice, this often meant that I only gave a few choices because the outcomes were more predictable. For example, in daily writing practice, I'd offer the following styles of exercises:

- ◆ I'd put a pile of random objects – tchotchkes, stuffed animals, toys, items I pulled from the trash – on the table, have students pick an object that spoke to them, and then describe it in 4 sentences. Everyone got a different object.
- ◆ I'd invite a special guest – like the librarian, my dog, or my friend's pet tarantula – to class. I asked the students to describe how the guest moved, sat, looked, and appeared. If students didn't want to write about the live guest, they could write about a person or creature they already knew.
- ◆ I'd send students outside with the instruction to "observe an object or situation of interest for 5 minutes and take notes". Then they'd come back to class and write a description of what they'd observed.

You may not be wowed by the fairly limited choices listed above, but I know these choices are effective because I've seen kids' eyes light up as they weigh their options and the zest with which they dig into the work. And, if you examine school through the lens of agency, you realize that so much of a student's day is characterized by *lack* of autonomy: they can't move about the room as they like; they can't sit where they prefer; they can't express themselves the way they are used to; and they can't even use the bathroom when they like! It's no surprise, then, that offering students choices like writing about an object they've selected confers a thrilling kind of freedom.

It's easy to offer more choices in long-term assignments or summative assessments. Consider the performance-based assessments I've used:

- ◆ Write about a mystery.
- ◆ Write about an adventure.
- ◆ Build a monster that represents your fear and write a story about that monster.
- ◆ Write about connection.
- ◆ Write about a character who does or does not have a purpose.

These were weeks-long assignments requiring the application of skills the students had built over time. The prompts were broad and the guidelines were few, which meant students could write in whatever format they preferred and they were free to interpret words like "adventure" and "monster" and "connection" however they liked.

Students wrote stories about family secrets, narratives detailing their adventures while skiing, love stories told in text messages, and opinion pieces about the value of friendship. Even with the "monster" prompt – which feels more constrained than the others – students drew, sculpted, molded, and animated their monsters. They wrote autobiographies, resumes, and how-to manuals about the monsters. Choice imbued the student's work with deep meaning and relevance, which in turn led to joy in its satisfactory execution.

For disciplines other than English, choice can look like the following:

◆ For the summative assessment, allow students to "complete 1 of the 3 following problems" that require the same knowledge and skill.
◆ If you have students memorize content, give them choices about which part of the content they'll produce at each assessment.
◆ In a presentation, give students the option of an audio or video recording as well as live presentations.
◆ Allow students to design their own experiments, even if it means they have to create the materials required for testing.

Considering Appropriate Challenges

As you design assignments, it's helpful to think about how the various choices impact the level of difficulty.[2] For example, in my interpretation of Bloom's Taxonomy (2011 version), creating something entirely new requires a higher order application of skill and knowledge than analyzing something that already exists (Armstrong). Therefore, writing a fictional story is a bit more challenging than writing a narrative or persuasive essay. As I talk with each student about their project, I explain the opportunities and challenges inherent in their intended approach, and, when asked, offer ways to make the work easier or even more challenging. This requires deep listening, as I don't want my suggestions to be biased by my own sense of what the student can handle. Instead, students opt in to challenges that appeal to them, and my job is to coach each student to success in that selected challenge. Sometimes that means I provide scaffolding by helping students break their projects into smaller chunks, and sometimes it means I read a page and simply confirm the student is headed in the right direction.

Examples of challenges my students have opted in to include:

- One student created artworks to accompany her story about connection. The art represented the various stages of friendship detailed in the story.
- Another student loved language and wanted to get all the vocabulary words she'd encountered in class into her written works. She managed to get about 80% of the class words into her projects, which was impressive.
- A student wanted to heighten his grammar skills, so he set himself the task of ensuring there were no sentence fragments in his papers all year. He accomplished his goal.
- Another student wanted to have a twist ending in each of his stories. He maintained his twist endings throughout the year and even included a twist in his final exam. Each ending was unique and didn't rely on tropes like, "it was all a dream".

These challenges made the work of English class engaging, even for students who didn't normally like reading or writing. In fact, one student who used to be bummed out by English class told me it became her favorite class. The reason, she said, was because she had the chance to explore different types of writing, push herself when she wanted to, and find success. The other benefit of the model of challenge I've proposed is that when these challenges are met, students experience the joy of mastering a skill that used to be difficult. It is gratifying to set and achieve a goal.

In disciplines other than English, challenge may be found in:

- Using the design thinking process to solve a problem in the student's own lives, like why they don't have matching socks or access to music they love at a reasonable price.
- Designing a prototype of a device that might address climate change, like a CO_2 vacuum.
- Writing word problems for classmates using the skills in the unit.
- Creating a game that teaches a concept covered in class, just as Monopoly teaches the ideas behind capitalism.

Applying the lenses of play, choice, and challenge[3] to the daily work of class helps you create assignments that kids want to engage in.

Summary

- ◆ Shifting curriculum, assessment, and grading requires a shift in instruction.
- ◆ Retool methods of instruction by applying the lenses of choice, challenge, and play.
- ◆ Use framing activities to set a positive tone and create the conditions for learning.
- ◆ Design activities, assignments, and assessments that can be tailored to students' skill level and interests

Notes

1 For those of you wondering, these mice completed the cycle of life by feeding the giant python in a 5th grade classroom.
2 As mentioned in Chapter 3, finding appropriate challenges is also how you individualize assignments and instruction.
3 Appendix B includes checklists and worksheets that guide you in application of the lenses of choice, challenge, and play.

Works Cited

Adams, Douglas. *Hitchhiker's Guide to the Galaxy*. Del Rey Books Mass Market Edition, 2005.

Armstrong, Patricia. "Bloom's Taxonomy". Vanderbilt University Center for Teaching. https://cft.vanderbilt.edu/guides-sub-pages/blooms-taxonomy/. Accessed 19 September 2022.

Baumeister, R. F., Vohs, K. D, Tice, D. M. "The Strength Model of Self-Control". *Current Directions in Psychological Science*. Vol 16, Issue 6, pp 351–355, 2007.

Golding, William. *Lord of the Flies*. Penguin Reissue Edition, 1959.

Rowling, J. K. *Harry Potter and the Philosopher's Stone*. Bloomsbury Press, 1997.

Tice Dianne, M., Baumeister, Roy F., Shmueli, Dikla and Muraven, Mark. "Restoring the Self: Positive Affect Helps Improve Self-Regulation Following Ego Depletion". *Journal of Experimental Social Psychology*. Vol 43, Issue 3, pp 379–384, 2007, ISSN 0022-1031.

7

Joyful Direction

My intention, as I write, is to make this the world's shortest chapter, and my reasoning is thus: any advice I might have about directing a classroom is almost worthless, because what works for me may not work for you. In fact, what works for me one day with one student may not work the next day with the same student! Consequently, my advice here is pretty simple:

> Different kids need different things. Deliver what each kid needs as required.

Ultimately, to be a successful director of a group of people, you should be a slightly more cheerful, patient version of yourself. Kids know when you're being phony and they deplore it. That's why many substitute teachers struggle. The best substitutes just lean into their role, saying, "Hey kids, your teacher is out and I'm here to try to prevent any catastrophes. That's my goal for today. What's yours?" And this kind of authenticity is required of every successful classroom teacher.

Obviously it's a significant challenge to deliver what every kid needs. Doing so means, #1, that you discover what each of your students need, and #2, that you have the bandwidth to provide what's needed. To accomplish #1, you'll need time and patience as you ferret out information about your students. You have to play games with them, read their work, ask them questions that don't feel nosy or gossipy but genuine, and observe them as they interact with others. You can also use Google Surveys to ask targeted questions about curriculum and instruction. To accomplish #2, you have to create

DOI: 10.4324/9781003374909-7

the time to touch base with every student almost every time class meets. That means structuring your class such that you aren't talking the entire time… instead, students should work together to practice the skills of your subject in some engaging fashion, leaving you the time to check in on each student and offering whatever feedback or support is needed. The connection you'll develop with your students by doing this leads to positive emotions, which in turn makes your class a place students want to be.

My final thought on this issue of directing the class is that if you fully engage your resources in #1 and #2, above, you won't have "management" issues. When students feel acknowledged, cared for, and provided with what they need to develop and grow, they tend to want to do their best. It's that simple. Meeting their needs doesn't mean that students won't ever blurt out thoughtless comments or roll around on the floor occasionally, but these moments shouldn't stress you out. It's not your job to prevent your students from having bursts of silliness or impulsivity, but it is your job to foster an environment in which children and adolescents can joyfully learn. The best way to do that is to approach your students with all the compassion, creativity, and joy you can muster.

With this being said, I present to you a summary of the advice I was either offered in my first years of teaching or that my teaching colleagues were offered. It's my version of *You're Wrong About* for teachers!

Common Advice	Why This Advice Is Flawed	What You Should Do Instead
Start the year super strict and then lighten up as the year progresses.	This advice undervalues authenticity and respect for the students. In what other job does someone say "be a jerk so that the people you're meant to lead are afraid of you"?	Start the year kind, open, flexible, and with good humor. Be yourself and respect students' rights to be themselves, too. Create a warm, supportive, inclusive environment by asking questions, playing games, allowing students choices, and providing as much student agency as possible.
Rules in the syllabus are sacrosanct.	No rule is sacrosanct. In fact, reasonable people can disagree and reasonable people with good intentions can write ludicrous rules.	Have students write the rules themselves and encourage them to limit the number of rules to three or four.

(continued)

Common Advice	Why This Advice Is Flawed	What You Should Do Instead
		In addition, recognize that we all have moments when our actions don't align with the values we hold for ourselves. Be compassionate as kids figure out how to align their behavior to their values.
All misbehavior should be called out and dealt with.	Not only is this humiliating to students, it's impossible to live up to and exhausting.	Ignore most mild misbehavior. When necessary, redirect students in a positive way with words of encouragement and gentle support, like, "We're talking about how different cultures have a god of time right now. What do you think about that?" Obviously, physical violence, hateful language (i.e., racist, sexist, homophobic), and microaggressions are different and require immediate intervention.
Late work should be punished by having points deducted.	Turning in work late happens for lots of reasons. Sometimes those reasons are within students' control and sometimes they are not. Regardless, punishments are not effective means of behavior change.	Assume that most of your students want to please you by doing their work on time. Explain that when you get the work, you can provide feedback, which is critical for authentic learning. Encourage students to turn in their work on time as a way to prevent a backlog. Accept late work without penalty or snarky comment.

Common Advice	Why This Advice Is Flawed	What You Should Do Instead
Effort can be judged by the teacher and should comprise a percentage of the grade.	Effort is completely subjective. What is effortful for one student is effortless for another, and the only person qualified to judge that effort is the student. Ergo, effort should not be part of a grade.	Work *product* should be assessed and quantified rather than work effort.
Homework should be assigned daily.	Work that requires fairly frequent teacher feedback shouldn't be done at home! For example, if you want students to practice a set of problems, that should be done at school so you can guide learning and prevent misunderstandings.	If you must assign homework, let it be the instruction, explanation, or demonstration you typically give in class, delivered via video. Or, homework can be reading that doesn't require your explanation.

Summary

- "Directing the class" strategies depend on the student and the situation.
- Learn everything you can about your students so you can deliver what each individual needs as they need it.
- A joyful classroom is infused with positive emotions like humor, optimism, curiosity, and enthusiasm.
- When you get advice, ask yourself, "How does this serve joyful student learning?"

Works Cited

Marshall, Sarah. *You're Wrong About*. Apple Podcasts, 2018.

Appendix A

A Note about Pushback

My daughter – who has newly entered the education profession – urged me to write this note about pushback you might encounter as you employ some of the tools I explain in this book. At her young age, she already understands that one of the hardest parts about teaching is dealing with other people's opinions about every decision you make. It can certainly be demoralizing.

Alas, I don't have a one-size-fits-all solution to complaints you might get about using, for example, a highest grade = term grade model. Each situation has variables that demand your attention and thoughtfulness. However, I can say this: marshalling supporting evidence helps your cause, as does citing improved outcomes in your students' performance. That means:

1   If you haven't already, familiarize yourself with the tenets and research mentioned in this book, especially around grading, as category grading systems are the norm and opposition to other systems is strong. The three books that are critical for understanding are by Joe Feldman, Ken O'Connor, and Thomas Guskey. Google these guys! They are experts and the evidence they provide is compelling.

2   Take notes and keep close track of your students' performance. Continually ask yourself, what have the kids learned and how do I know they have learned it? Survey the students frequently about their experience and use their feedback to improve. The very best "proof of concept" is when your students do well, but don't just rely on your intuition that they've done well. Collect and use data as much as possible, without turning into a robot about it.

Additionally, when your teaching partners are reluctant to adopt a particular instructional mode or grading practice, it might be helpful to ask if you could try the method for a set period of time. If the method is unsuccessful at the end of the time period, then you could try something else. As an example, if students choosing their own books makes your teaching partner nervous, ask if you can try *one unit* in which students choose their own books. Most of the time, people will agree to try a practice if they know they don't have to do it forever. And, when teachers see that a particular practice improves results – while also generating more motivated, enthusiastic students – they are more likely to continue that routine.

Ultimately, the methods and practices I've described in this book are student-centered, inclusive, equitable, and collaborative. There isn't much to push back on in that line up, so move forward knowing that your goal is a connected, dedicated, joyful community of learners.

Appendix B

Checklists and Extras

Planning a Year Checklist

	To Do
	Write five broad learning targets, understanding that there will be sub-skills and knowledge embedded in the broad targets
	Use your learning targets to write an essential question or series of essential questions
	Use your learning targets to backwards plan the assessments and assignments
	Look at your assessments and assignments through the lens of choice
	Look at your assessments and assignments through the lens of challenge
	Look at your assessments and assignments through the lens of play

Learning Targets Worksheet

1	Brainstorm a list of what you want students to **know** and **be able to do** by the end of the year. Put aside **work habits** and just focus on the skills and content areas of your grade/discipline. To be clear, work habits are things like "Collaborates with others to find a solution" or "Turns in work on time" or "Organizes binder appropriately".
2	Imagine your students at the end of the school year. What are the top five skills from the brainstormed list they need to have? In other words, what are the five **essential** skills/understandings of your discipline?

3	Write the top five skills as learning targets, which you do by putting the skill after the words "I can".
	Examples of Learning Targets
	I can use the FOIL method to multiply binomials.
	I can write a lab report using six steps.
	I can use accurate Spanish to ask for directions.
	I can develop a thesis about a historical event.
	I can write an essay with a big idea in mind.
	I can choreograph two minutes of a dance.
	I can draw a picture of a figure.
	I can sing using accurate pitch.
4	Look at what you wrote for #3. What are the sub-skills embedded in those learning targets? Write learning targets for those sub-skills.

5	Assess: what is missing from your learning target lists? Look back at your brainstormed list for inspiration. Write any other learning targets here, but keep the number under 20 total, if at all possible. Remember, you have to write a rubric for every learning target!
6	Lastly, put your learning targets in the order they should be mastered.

Writing Essential Questions

1	Review your learning target list and remind yourself about the top five.
2	For each of the top five learning targets, consider: what are the steps students must take to master those skills? Sketch it out, below.
3	Look at the steps you just detailed. Write a few questions that could guide students from one step to the next.

4	Now, look at the questions you just wrote. What broader question can you ask about the subject matter of your class that invites critical thinking and propels deeper investigation/understanding? Brainstorm options.
5	Look at your work in #4. Which of those questions captures the big idea of your class? That's the essential question around which you can focus your assessments and assignments.

Backwards Planning

1	Get out your list of learning targets
2	How many grading terms are in your year? Consider how you'll divide the presentation of learning targets across the terms, being mindful of appropriate scaffolding.
3	Create a list of learning targets by grading term.
4	Now, plan the summative assessments for each term based on the learning targets. **Reminders** ◆ Students will find more success if you focus on a few learning targets at a time. ◆ Consider how your assessment contributes to the students' understanding of the essential question. ◆ How can you develop performance-based assessments that ask students to use the skills they've practiced? For example, if the skill is percentages, can you create a situation in which students would have to "shop" for items on discount or figure out how to reduce a recipe?

5	Once you have the summative assessments planned, think about the smaller assignments that lead up to each summative assessment… the formative assessments. Look again at the learning targets and consider the steps students take to master those learning targets…the progression of learning. Plan assignments that will guide students to progress in their mastery of the targeted skill.

Reminders

- ◆ Assignments can be daily work done in class, or smaller projects that take a few weeks to complete
- ◆ These assignments should build in complexity until the summative assessment
- ◆ Assignments should focus on one learning target at a time

Apply the Lens of Choice

1	Create a list of the summative assessments you plan for each grading term.
2	For each assessment, consider the choices you can offer students about their final product that allows for a variety of learners. For example, some kids love to build things with their hands, while others like to create presentations. Allow students to show you what they know and can do in a way that suits their interests and talents. Make sure each choice meets the learning targets.
3	Write down the options you'll provide for each assessment.

4	Now, repeat steps 1–3 for the practice assignments. The choices offered in the practice should echo the choices offered in the summative assessments.

Apply the Lens of Challenge

1	Look at your list of summative assessments and assignments and the choices you've come up with for students.
2	Examine each summative assessment through the lens of challenge by looking at the choices. Can each assessment be scaled up in intensity/difficulty for students seeking to challenge themselves? Can each assessment be scaled down in intensity/difficulty for students who need more support?
3	Make adjustments to the choices based on your review.
4	Repeat steps 1–3 for the practice assignments.

Apply the Lens of Play

1	Look at your list of summative assessments and assignments including the choices and challenges you've designed.
2	For the summative assessments, consider how you can infuse each one with a playful spirit. Performance-based assessment is definitely a good start toward playfulness, so reflect on how you can create performance-based assessments. If nothing springs to mind, consider adding game elements or a simulation to the assessment scenario.
3	For the practice assignments, again consider performance-based work. Then, think about how to add play to each assignment through games, simulations, dramatic re-enactments, music, art, and sport or other physical movement. Alternatively, consider how to create a context for the practice assignment by using play. One note here: students already spend a lot of time on screens. Whatever play you add to their assignments should be analog in nature.

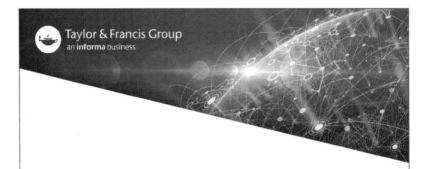

For Product Safety Concerns and Information please contact our
EU representative GPSR@taylorandfrancis.com Taylor & Francis
Verlag GmbH, Kaufingerstraße 24, 80331 München, Germany